WORDS OF WAR

Jack Cahill

DENEAU

DENEAU PUBLISHERS & COMPANY LTD.
760 BATHURST STREET
TORONTO, ONTARIO
M5S 2R6

© 1987

Typesetting: Computer Composition of Canada, Inc.

Printed in Canada

Jack Cahill photos courtesy of *The Toronto Star*.

Passage on pages 42-43 reprinted by permission of the Associated Press; on pages 121-124 by permission of United Press International; on pages 55-93 by permission of the *London Sunday Times*.

Passage on page 102 from *Murder of a Gentle Land* by John Barron and Anthony Paul, New York: Readers' Digest Press, 1977. Reprinted by permission of McGraw-Hill Book Company; from *From Our Special Correspondent* by Robert Wilkinson-Latham on pages xv, xvi, xviii, xix by permission of Hodder & Stoughton Limited, Mill Road, Dunton Green, Sevenoaks, Kent.

This book has been published with the assistance of the Canada Council and Ontario Arts Council under their block grant programmes.

Canadian Cataloguing in Publication Data
Cahill, Jack
Words of War
Includes index
ISBN 0-88879-146-1 (bound). – ISBN 0-88879-148-8 (pbk.)
1. Cahill, Jack. 2. Foreign correspondents – Vietnam – Biography. 3. Foreign correspondents – Cambodia – Biography. 4. Vietnamese Conflict, 1961-1975 – Personal narratives. 5. Vietnam – Description and travel – 1975- . I. Title.
DS559.5.C33 1987   959.704'38   C87-093232-2

To Neil Davis –

who covered one story too many.

CHINA

Hanoi ✪

Halong

Haiphong

LAOS

VIETNAM

Gulf of Tonkin

Hue

THAILAND

Danang

KAMPUCHEA
(CAMBODIA)

Ho Chi Minh City
(Saigon)

Gulf of Siam

South China Sea

The Toronto Star

Map of Vietnam.

Contents

Acknowledgments

MOST OF MY THANKS FOR HELP with this book must go to my colleagues of the later stages of the Indochina wars, who helped me initially with their company and advice and eventually with their anecdotes. If ageing legs will carry me to any more crises I owe a lift "up the road" or a lead on a story especially to Tony Paul, of *Readers' Digest*, and Jon Swain of *The London Sunday Times*. I'd do the same if I could for Neil Davis of NBC, but he covered one story too many and is not with us any more.

For my research into other wars of the Victorian era I depended greatly on the work of Robert Wilkinson-Latham, whose book, *From Our Special Correspondent*, was published in Britain by Hodder and Staughton in 1979. And for my understanding of the coverage of World Wars I and II, I am mainly indebted to Phillip Knightley, whose classic on war correspondents, *The First Casualty*, was published by Harcourt Brace Jovanovich in 1975. I also owe thanks to the McGraw-Hill Book Company for permission to use a passage from *Murder of a Gentle Land* by Jon Barron and

Anthony Paul published in 1977; to *The London Sunday Times* for permission to use Jon Swain's story on the fall of Phnom Penh; and, of course, to *The Toronto Star* which paid my way to most of the places I went and published my stories, some of which have been condensed or expanded in this book.

Words of War would not have happened, however, unless my literary agent and friend, Beverley Slopen, along with a considerable and surprising number of other people, had asked me to try to keep the spirit of my earlier book alive. A special person among this group was Doris Giller, the former book editor for the Montreal Gazette. I am also grateful to Sandra Tooze, the editor of this book.

Parts of *Words of War,* now rewritten and updated, appeared in my 1980 book, titled *If You Don't Like the War, Switch the Damn Thing Off!* That was more of a personal memoir than a look at the occurrences of the last years of the Vietnam and Cambodia wars and the correspondents who covered them, as this book is. The world has changed since 1980, Indochina with it, and it is my belief that people are beginning to realize, belatedly, the horrors of the Cambodian holocaust. The American people especially are ready now to look at Vietnam, not as a national disgrace to be switched off their media and from their minds, but as a place and time that should be worthy again of their attention. At least, those were the thoughts of American Vietnam veterans with whom I returned to that unfortunate country in 1986 for the purpose of writing this book.

Introduction

THEY WERE A DIFFERENT KIND OF MAN. There was adventure in them and curiosity and a perverse and sometimes devilish anti-establishment attitude. And they were driven by a need to communicate what was really going on in a world full of myths, images and propaganda.

Often they took great risks and endured much hardship in their difficult line of business and some of them died. They drank a lot and smoked cigars and they were bound together in a camaraderie that is known only to those who suffer the grimmest of experiences and run the risk of death together.

The first of them was a lawyer named Henry Crabb Robinson, whom *The Times of London* sent to cover the Napoleonic Wars in Central Europe in 1807. He produced a series of letters headlined "From the Banks of the Elbe." However, he was not much good as a war correspondent. He tended to base his reports on what he read in the local newspapers rather than on personal observation. In his last dispatch from Corruna, in January 1809 after the French had been repulsed, he failed to even mention the death of the British commander-in-chief, Sir John Moore. When the British troops left the Spanish mainland, Robinson returned to England and wisely abandoned journalism to resume his career as a lawyer.

But many other more successful "special correspondents" followed him into this adventurous occupation. They covered the wars in the Crimea, Sudan, Abyssinia, America, Europe, the Pacific, Indochina, and a lot of smaller wars in between. Some of them—Winston Churchill was one—cared almost entirely about the military aspects of war, as if it was a game, some of them were adventurers who liked the excitement of the "bang bangs" and some were humanists who sometimes got sick and often got scared.

This book is about some of the correspondents in the Indochina wars, what they saw, what they wrote and what happened to them. But first it is necessary to understand that the Indochina correspondents were a part of a tradition of freedom, objectivity and independence that first flourished in the Victorian era, was dropped for a while during World Wars I and II, resumed again to an extent in the Korean War of the 1950s and then fully restored in Cambodia and Vietnam in the 1960s and 1970s.

The campaigns of the old hands of the Victorian era have been chronicled by Robert Wilkinson-Latham in a volume called *From Our Special Correspondent—Victorian War Correspondents and Their Campaigns* (Hodder and Stoughton, 1979). The similarities between the way they operated and the professional attitudes and behaviour of today's correspondents are obvious and interesting.

Today's correspondents are harrassed. Around the world in 1985, twenty-three were killed, eighty-one wounded and 205 jailed. This is worse than it has ever been but it is not new. During the Carlist war in Spain in

1837, for instance, *The Morning Post* sent C.L. Gruneisen, who was better known as a music critic, while *The Times* employed a Captain Henningsen. Both of them were captured and deported from Spain after one Spanish general proclaimed that Gruneisen had done more harm with his pen than any of the Carlist generals with their swords, and that he would have no compunction at all about shooting all Carlist correspondents.

George Borrow, in his book *The Bible in Spain*, described the correspondents of the English press at that time as "cosmopolites."

The activity, energy and courage they display are truly remarkable [he wrote]. *I saw them during three days in Paris* [1830] *mingle with the* canaille *and rabble behind the barriers . . . . There they stood, dotting down what they saw in their notebooks as unconcerned as if reporting a Reform meeting in Finsbury Square or Covent Garden, while in Spain they accompanied the Carlist and Christino guerrillas on some of their most desperate expeditions, sleeping on the ground, exposing themselves fearlessly to hostile bullets, to the inclemency of the winter and the fierce rays of summer's burning sun.*

They were always in trouble, these curious nineteenth century men who risked their necks for news. The army brass often obstructed them. The bugs bit and the bullets killed. And the censors were strict, although beatable with slyness and skill. Rudyard Kipling wrote that the correspondents of this Victorian era did not just have to be good observers and writers but also needed ". . . the constitution of a bullock, the digestion of an ostrich and an infinite adaptability to all circumstances."

But when they could they looked after themselves as well as possible, a tradition also followed by their successors in Indochina. One of the best of them, Melton Prior, who wrote and sketched for the *Illustrated London News* arrived on the west coast of Africa in 1873 with baggage containing a fifty-pound case of preserved meat, rice and biscuits, plus a sixty-pound case of claret and whisky, along with the usual tents, wagons, servants and porters. He disguised his whisky in boxes marked "drawing materials." In the Sudan in the 1890s, a favorite line of Ernest Bennett, of the *Westminster Gazette* was, "When the whisky mule halts, it is kindness to lighten his burden."

And when Winston Churchill, who went on to other things, left to cover the Boer War in 1899 he had shipped aboard the *Dunottar Castle* with him the following from his wine merchant, Rudolph Payne and Sons:

6 October, 1899   61 St. James's Street S.W.

	£	s.	d.
6 Bottles 1889 Vin d'Ay Sec	2	15	0
18 Bottles St. Emilion	1	16	0
6 Bottles light Port	1	1	0
6 Bottles French Vermouth	0	18	0
18 Bottles Scotch Whiskey (10 years old)	3	12	0
6 Bottles Very Old Eau de Vie (landed 1866)	4	0	0
12 Rose's Cordial Lime Juice	0	15	0
6 × 1 dozen cases for same, packing, marking, etc.	0	10	0
Cartage, dock charges and insurance	0	13	0
TOTAL	16	0	0

Sent by SS *Dunottar Castle* to South Africa

Communications were far from instant for these old-timers, as they can often be today if the correspondent is not near a wire service, telephone or satellite dish. In the beginning, dispatches came from Europe by ship to Plymouth and were taken by coach or rider to London. Brief details of very important news were sent to London by "telegraphic" dispatch, which was a system of sending signals with flags from post to post, usually hilltops in sight of each other. In India much use was made of the heliograph, a system of signalling with mirrors and sunlight. Then in 1844 an artist and portrait photographer named F.B. Morse invented his code and opened his first telegraph line between Baltimore and Washington; a system that was to link whole continents within the next few decades so that news could then travel faster than a horse could run or even the newfangled trains could rattle. Submarine cables linked continents by the mid-1850s and Alexander Graham Bell revolutionized communications with his invention of the telephone in 1876. But the telephone was seldom used by correspondents then and remained little used by the modern correspondents until recently, when the small portable computer that plugs into a phone and transmits printed words was invented.

Then, as also now, the correspondents were seldom close to the source of any system of communication so they used daring dispatch riders, who were paid handsomely for their risks. "A dispatch rider," wrote Fred W. Unger, a correspondent for the *Daily Express* during the Boer War, "gets nearly a pound a mile but as often as not he does not get very far. Only the other day four of Reuter's dispatch riders were caught by the Boers near Mafeking." Instead, in Indochina, the correspondents used an informal co-operative system called "pigeoning" in which they would carry even a dreaded rival's copy or film to the transmission point when they had to go there themselves.

The greatest of the correspondents of the early era was William Howard Russell, an Irishman, who worked for the *Times of London*. In the Crimea, Russell was the first correspondent to write about war the way it really was, to describe death and horror, and also to be critical of the army of his own country. He denounced the management of the British Army for crass inefficiency and described the unsanitary conditions the troops were subjected to and the diarrhoea and cholera those conditions caused. He was a colourful character, dressed usually in a commissariat officer's cap with gold lace band, a rifleman's patrol jacket, cord breeches, boots and spurs.

Sometimes he wrote almost poetically. From Varnia during the Crimean War, after visiting a British camp that had become known as "The Valley of Death," he wrote:

The meadows nurtured the fever [cholera]*, the ague, dysentry and pestilence in their bosum—the lake and the stream exhaled death, and at night fat, unctious vapors rose ... from the valley and crept in the dark and stole into the tent of the sleeper and wrapped him in their deadly embrace.*

And about his own circumstances at Gallipoli in 1854, he wrote:

I run a good chance of starving. ... I have no tent nor can I get one without an order and even if I had one I doubt very much whether Sir George [Brown] *would allow me to pitch it within the camp. ... I am now living in a pigsty, without chair, table, stool or window glass. ... I live on eggs and brown bread, sour Tenedos wine, and onions and rice. ...*

Obviously, Russell's vivid style of journalism and detailed descriptive passages, including the frequent, bitter portrayals of an archaic and outdated military system, aroused public opinion in Britain. They almost literally upset the government. So did a habit of the correspondents of occasionally looking at both sides of a war and even praising the bravery of the enemy "natives," in particular the "fuzzy-wuzzy" dervishes of the Sudan.

I don't know how it is [wrote a Colonel Somerset Clathorpe] *but the reporters of the English journals have made themselves very unpopular. They appear to try to find fault wherever they can, and throw as much blame and contempt on the English authorities as if their object was to bring the British Army into disrepute with our allies.*

Russell was, in fact, a courageous hero who could write. During his many wars he was awarded five campaign medals and six foreign orders. He was knighted in 1895 and his epitaph in St. Paul's Cathedral states that he was "the first and greatest of war correspondents."

The many who followed him in the wars of the Victorian era included the American Henry Morton Stanley, of the *New York Herald*, whose first overseas campaign was the Abyssinian War in the 1860s, where he injected a bit of American brashness into the business.

Before he arrived in Abyssinia, Stanley called at the telegraph office in Suez and greased the palm of the head telegraphist to make sure his dispatches would get preference. And then, after the fall of Magdala, while the British correspondents made a fairly leisurely way towards the coast, Stanley hurried to catch the first ship up the Red Sea towards Suez and the telegraph line. He found that the official dispatches about the end of the war were being carried in the same ship so that his chances of a world-wide scoop were remote. Although he would beat his British rivals, the newspapers would print the government announcement. But luck was with Stanley, as it often is with the reporter who tries hardest. An outbreak of cholera occurred on board and the ship was placed in quarantine, along with the official dispatches. Stanley smuggled his report ashore with a note to the bribed head telegraphist and the telegram was sent to London and relayed to New York where the *Herald* immediately published it. Then when the official dispatches were eventually released, the telegrapher broke all rules by putting Stanley's follow-up story on the wire ahead of them. Just as the telegrapher had finished tapping out the last words of this story, the submarine cable between Alexandria and Malta broke, preventing the British correspondents from getting their news to London. As a result of this scoop Stanley was given a roving commission by his paper, and became immortal when he found Dr. Livingston in the jungles of Africa in 1872.

Stanley had cut his correspondent's teeth in the American Civil War of the 1860s, which was the first war to be covered by correspondents in vast numbers. There were about five hundred Americans writing from the northern side alone as well as representatives of the London and other foreign presses, including, of course, the ever-present Russell of *The Times*.

It was also the first war between conventional armies that was extensively covered by war photographers, the precursors of today's television cameramen. John MacCosh, a surgeon in the British Bengal Army is credited by the historian Wilkinson-Latham as being the first war photographer. He took small portraits of officers and men during the Second Sikh War (1848-49) using clumsy photographic processes first invented in 1839, and during the Second Burma War (1853-54) he photographed the captured cities of Rangoon and Prome. But these were set, static pictures and none of his work or that of other early war photographers showed the horrors or sufferings of war. The first photographer to do this was Felice Beato, a Venetian by birth and naturalized British subject, who produced remarkable pictures showing the destruction and desolation caused by the Indian Mutiny, and later recorded the Second China War in 1860 with its terrible havoc and death.

But in the American Civil War a man named Matthew Brady really brought war photography into fashion. He employed twenty-two teams of photographers and assistants whose many graphic pictures brought the aftermath of battle, with the hundreds of dead and dying, into the living rooms of America. These photos tarnished the romantic image of war, as Russell had done with his colourful writings from Crimea and television cameramen were to do years later in Vietnam. But Brady was only able to do this belatedly because none of the illustrated newspapers of the day could reproduce his work. His pictures were not massively circulated until the early 1880s, fifteen years after the war, when the halftone process for printing photographs was perfected. By that time, although the realism of the pictures still startled and shocked, they were too late to have any political effect on the war as the film and photographs from Vietnam did. It was also too late for Brady. He died in a New York poor ward.

There were censors, of course, in the Victorian era but they were part of the game and the correspondents often frustrated and defeated them. For instance, when the British government decided in 1902 that a negotiated peace was necessary in the Boer War and concluded it with the Treaty of Vereeniging, correspondents were excluded from the peace discussions. But Edgar Wallace, of the *London Daily Mail,* arranged with one of the soldiers guarding the Vereeniging camp to signal him when the peace was signed. Wallace travelled back and forth past the camp in a train, waiting for the signal to come. On one of the passes the soldier blew his nose with a white handkerchief. So Wallace wired the *Daily Mail,* "Have bought you 1,000 Rand Collieries"—an inoffensive message that passed the censors but tipped the *Daily Mail* to the end of the war even before the news reached the government. The newspaper locked its entire production and editorial staff in its Carmelite House offices the night before publication to protect its scoop. Wallace was subsequently informed by Lord Kitchener, a notorious press hater who led the British campaign in South Africa, that he would not be allowed to act as a war correspondent again because he had evaded the rules of censorship. Wallace laughed and went on to write novels.

But this sort of independence was not possible in World Wars I and II when censorship was extremely strict, especially after America entered World War II and public relations became an important part of the Allied military machine. (By late 1944 the Allied public relations headquarters in Paris had the staff and facilities to censor, slant or occasionally pass each week more than three million words from nearly 1,000 correspondents, plus 35,000 photographs and 100,000 feet of newsreel film.) In these wars the correspondents covered the activities of their own friendly and supportive armies often bravely, but with uncritical patriotism. They were given honorary commissions, wore officers' uniforms and were essentially a part of the act rather than observers of it. Only a very few, like the

Australian Keith Murdoch, father of the present media baron Rupert Murdoch, ever dared to defy the censorship system. He broke the story of the disastrous Allied situation at Gallipoli in 1915, but only after being held in custody and having his story confiscated. He wrote it from memory after his release.

In the circumstances few of the correspondents of the Great Wars made any claim to objectivity. "The first casualty when war comes is truth," said American senator Hiram Johnson in 1917. And Charles Lynch, the Canadian World War II correspondent admitted thirty years after that war: "It's humiliating to look back at what we wrote during the war. It was crap—and I don't exclude the Ernie Pyles and the Alan Mooreheads. We were a propaganda arm of our governments. At the start the censors enforced that, but by the end we were our own censors. We were cheerleaders. I suppose there wasn't an alternative at the time. It was total war. But for God's sake, let's not glorify our role. It wasn't good journalism. It wasn't journalism at all."

So it was not until the Indochina wars of the 1960s and 1970s and the coincident troubles in the Middle East and Central and South America that the correspondents reverted again to the freewheeling, more objective, sometimes critical style of William Howard Russell, Henry Morton Stanley and their colleagues of the Victorian era.

Now the correspondents began again to report on both sides of the wars when they could, and often both sides were unfriendly. The contact in the field was no longer a helpful GI or a cool British officer but frequently an excited, uneducated fifteen-year-old kid carrying all the authority of an automatic weapon, often bigger than he was. And the important person to be interviewed was no longer a lucid Winston Churchill or a publicity-conscious General

Douglas McArthur, but often an illogical dictator like Idi Amin or Muammar Ghadafi, who was convinced that the Western correspondent was part of a Zionist plot and respected him somewhat less than the scores of his own countrymen he had killed in his rise to power.

Times again became tough, dangerous, uncertain and scary for the correspondents. They became an endangered species. A lot of them died.

1

The New Chums

HONG KONG IS A CROWD, a constant noise, a babble of bargaining, a sweatshop, a stock market, a gamble, a stink, a frightening big wind in the typhoon season.

It is also the blue waters lapping into little peaceful coves, the view from Victoria Peak over the wide Pacific Ocean, the serenity of Chinese grandmothers, walking hand in hand with well-dressed little kids in the parks.

Hong Kong is the *Hakka* ladies, their backs temporarily and their legs permanently bent as they carry big loads of bricks in baskets on busy construction sites, and millionaires' wives at the symphony concerts at city hall. It is pink Rolls Royces parked next to rickshaws, noodle stores in the streets next to elegant French restaurants, Buddhist temples and Catholic cathedrals, mansions surrounded by squatters' shacks, and sleek company yachts moored beside poor, unpainted little junks on which big families live all their lives.

This was our home base when I covered the Far East and South East Asia, a good base for a foreign correspondent because the press there was reasonably free—one of the very few parts of the world where this is the case these days—the communications good, and the living reasonably comfortable. There were about eighty of us correspondents in Hong Kong throughout the seventies; mostly American, of course, because they still control the news and slant it, but also British, German, Italian, French, Scandinavian, a few Canadians, some Australians who worked for non-Australian organizations, and late in the piece some Japanese.

It was just a base. The news was generally elsewhere, in the grim wars of Indochina, the remarkable economic miracles of Japan, Korea and Taiwan, the talkative turmoil of India, the troubles of the Third World, even the emergence of Papua New Guinea as an independent nation and dramatic elections in Australia. But Hong Kong was an interesting place to call home.

The people of Hong Kong worship the dollar. They also burn joss sticks in the streets and sweep the graves of their ancestors religiously every *Ching Ming* day. They built huge, modern, chrome and glass skyscrapers, then place mirrors on all the windows to deflect the *fung shui*— the evil spirits.

Police station sergeants become millionaires in Hong Kong from payoffs from the brothels and gambling joints. The firemen expect "tea money," often in substantial amounts, otherwise not only will they refuse to extinguish a fire in your home or business, they might start one. I had a few drinks one night with the British chief of the Royal Hong Kong Police Force's Triad (Chinese Mafia) squad and a BBC crew who were doing a documentary on him titled "Hong Kong's Honest Cop." The next afternoon the honest cop was arrested for corruption, thus putting a considerable damper on the BBC project.

Yet in Hong Kong the daughters of the *gweilos* (foreign devils) can walk anywhere, unmolested, at any time of the day or night.

You can buy anything on this little island and in its adjacent New Territories if you have the money and more than a tourist's acquaintance, from the oddest of sexual services to an air force of second-hand fighter planes. If you care to venture into the Walled City of Kowloon, where the buildings are so tall and the muddy streets so narrow the light never reaches the ground, you can arrange to equip an army or shoot a fix into a million arms. But you shouldn't go there unless you are known to the street vendors outside the only two entrances. The throats of all strangers, including policemen, are consistently slit.

Hong Kong should not work, but it does. The thousands of refugees who pour over the border every year, seeking a better life among the five million people already crowded into four square miles, should not be able to find homes and jobs and a better life, but somehow they do.

The deep ideological differences between the many Chinese in the colony who were Maoists and now follow the more pragmatic philosophies of Deng Xiaoping, the far-right British *Tai Pans* (who are in many cases their capitalistic, expatriate employers), the Chinese millionaires and stockmarket gamblers and the poor, shuffling labourers and boat people, should cause riots in the streets, but they don't or at least haven't since the Great Proletarian Cultural Revolution in China in 1967.

Now Hong Kong is to be turned back to the Chinese by 1997, so an atmosphere of uncertainty hovers even more ominously than before. But it always was uncertain, a borrowed place living on borrowed time. Without the excitement of uncertainty its industries would become ordinary, its people complacent and it would die.

Meanwhile the Chinese big businessmen with their

3

chauffeured Mercedes or Rolls Royces (a few of them gold plated), their huge shipping lines and portfolios of some of the world's most expensive real estate in Hong Kong and abroad, manage to maintain remarkably adaptable dual loyalties, buttering their bread on both sides of the border, ignoring ideologies in their scramble for more and more money.

Ho Yin is an example of these businessmen. He operates mainly in the tiny neighbouring allegedly-Portuguese colony of Macao, which is a gambling joint, Asia's Las Vegas, an incongruous pimple of ultracapitalism on the rump of Communist China. Macao is even more under Communist control than is Hong Kong and only forty-five minutes away by fast, efficient, capitalist-operated hydrofoil services.

Ho Yin owns Macao's electricity company, the jai alai court and the dog track, among other things, including eleven cars and one of the world's richest collections of jade. He is also a respected member of the Communist People's Congress in Beijing.

A colleague once asked Ho Yin, in a rare interview, how he could possibly reconcile all of his personal power and riches with communism.

"I'm not good enough to be a Communist," he replied.

It was always good to get home to Hong Kong, especially from places like Cambodia and Vietnam. The aircraft aims straight at a big black and white square painted on a hill near Kai Tak airport, swerves suddenly through a ninety-degree turn and swoops frighteningly between tall apartment buildings, with the inevitable washing hanging from

4

the balconies, until it bounces on the long runway. If it is not the most difficult landing in the world, it is at least the most exciting.

Sometimes, as the plane taxied along the strip that juts out into the "fragrant harbour" which gives the island its name, I could see my own little sloop through the window. It was moored safely among the junks and sampans at Kellett Island, where the *gweilos* sip their long, cool, drinks at the Royal Hong Kong Yacht Club, incongruously near a huge cluster of ugly harbour tenders crowded with Chinese families who live on them, seldom stepping ashore.

Usually there was a period of impatience to get home as we drove a few blocks to the Cathay Pacific cargo hut to ship rolls of film to Canada, waiting while the clerk laboriously typed out the bill of lading in English, then demanded my Chinese "chop"—or signature—so it could be sent home collect.

The Chinese characters representing my Irish name on my carved ivory chop translated vaguely into "expectations of excellence." It worked. The film was always sent collect.

Then the big Mercedes taxi would crawl through the thick traffic of Kowloon, past the street stalls with their dead ducks hanging among the colourful plastics and clothing and the ivory carvings, past the pharmacies with their varieties of wines—from five-mice wine with the five little white pickled bodies in the bottle, to silkworm-sperm wine. Good, the label says, for impotence and nocturnal emissions. Then through the area of textile factories where the big guillotines cut huge piles of denim into jeans by the millions, and little old ladies sew several different brand names onto products that pour from the same machines to fill the store shelves of the world.

The big car picked up speed in the tunnel under the

harbour and slowed again on the Hong Kong side in the hustle and smell of narrow Queen Street, near the big People's Republic Store, where you can buy anything from the mainland from works of art to cheap cashmere sweaters and frozen donkey legs; past the snake shops where the big, live cobras wait in wire cages to have their stomachs slit and their biles neatly squeezed into bowls of rice wine to make a concoction guaranteed to keep a Chinese warm all through a winter.

The way wound through the university area, a bunch of buildings on either side of Pokfulam Road, and eventually up a big hill. We lived in a huge, old, white stucco house on a pocket of land carved out of a mountainside so steep it seemed to hover over the flat roof, ready to fall at any time. Once when I was in Malaysia the Canadian Commission had a somewhat panicky call from my wife, Marie, saying it had done just that during a typhoon. In fact the mountain had only slid a bit against the back of the house near the maid's quarters, almost burying our maid in the process and sending the family scuttling to the Hilton Hotel for a few days.

The outside of the house was covered by an ugly, green, slimy fungus that grows long and lush in the high humidity, but inside it was palatial. Built in 1946 by a Chinese millionaire for his bride, it was a mausoleum of rich wood, winding staircases, and chandeliers. The ceilings were fifteen feet high, the living room big enough to hold a ball, and the master bedroom upstairs was forty feet long and thirty feet wide. The two main rooms were dominated by huge and ancient chandeliers, which our landlord, who owned two Rolls Royces, ran many low-wage enterprises, and professed Christianity, forced us to buy for five hundred dollars when we first rented the place.

When the proposition was first put I cabled the *Star*

asking for the money and received a reply weeks after we'd paid for them and moved in.

"We have checked and found the *Star* has no official policy about the purchase of antique chandeliers by correspondents," the reply said sternly and apparently seriously. "You will have to pay for them yourself."

After four months packed into two rooms at the Repulse Bay Hotel with the four kids, at a time when accommodation of any sort was virtually unavailable in the crowded colony, we were lucky to get one of the only houses for rent in Hong Kong for the chandelier-key money and two thousand dollars a month, which was about the average price of a good foreign-devil apartment.

Although the outside hadn't seen a coat of paint in at least a decade and the creaky big iron gates to the entrance courtyard were constantly falling off their hinges, the place had a little yard, a great rarity in Hong Kong. It looked out over the harbour at the point where the *Queen Elizabeth* caught fire and burned in 1972. She was being cut to bits by salvage crews at the beginning of our residence, until the big hulk eventually disappeared altogether.

The *Daily Telegraph* correspondent, who lived in a nearby apartment, received a phone call from his London office the day the liner sank asking if the big story was on the way.

"Hang on a sec, old chap, until I look out the window," he told the editor. Then after a pause the reporter's embarrassed voice told London: "By Jove, you're right, you know. The damn thing has sunk."

Chinese squatters lived on the mountain next to our big house and we believed, by the size of our bills, that they tapped our water and electricity supplies. They lived fairly well in their little shanties and were good, quiet neighbours. One of them, we suspected, was a leftover from the Japanese invasion of World War II because he exercised, with military precision and what looked like a rifle, every morning in front of his cave. Then he dressed in a neat blue business suit and set off for work, apparently in a downtown office.

By the time we arrived in Hong Kong in 1973, the traditional Chinese *amah,* or the live-in combination of *amah* and cook-boy, had practically priced themselves off the servants' market. Like many other expatriates, we imported two maids from the Philippines. Our housekeeper was an attractive, intelligent young woman from Mindanao, named Nazaria, who was paid in the beginning HK$450 (ninety US dollars) a month. Our "makee learnee" (apprentice) was her cousin Melinda who was paid about half that amount.

In the circumstances Marie didn't cook for almost five years and all meals we ate at home tasted of soya sauce even after we took to hiding the bottle from the two girls. And I wore, I believe, the same set of underwear for months at a time because as soon as I took it off it was washed and put back on top of the pile.

The kids were chauffered in a *pak pai,* an unlicensed, illegal taxi, to the excellent Hong Kong International School by a driver they nicknamed the Assassin in honour of the huge numbers of Chinese he scattered in the narrow streets. They never learned how to make a bed or wash a dish, but they made up for their lack of practical training, we believed, by completely failing in the end to see any difference between people of different races.

The Asian maid business, however, is not entirely the luxury it might seem to hardworking housewives in big homes in parts of the world where high wages have made house servants impossible.

Our girls became part of our already large family and thus they brought Marie their troubles: the brother arrested as a terrorist on Mindanao, the sister who needed money to build a house in Manila, what to wear to Mass, and how to help a Filipino friend who was pregnant. The tears and emotions made the "Missie's" executive and human responsibilities almost as arduous as housework itself.

And there were not only the maids but the old gardener who went with the house but was so old he could hardly walk, let alone work, and the garbage lady who had to be paid to take away the rubbish which she promptly sold to somebody else. Down at the yacht club there was Tamoy, the boat girl, who had to be employed (for fifty US dollars a month) so the sloop wouldn't be robbed or wrecked by whatever boat-boy Triad she had to pay for protection.

Almost all of the eighty or so correspondents in Hong Kong owned a boat or a share in one. They were mostly diesel-powered junks with their own permanent boat-boy, who did all the work, the sailing and the cooking while the "masters" and their families lounged about on deck with a glass of gin or swam in the clean waters of the outlying islands.

One TV reporter even managed to have his huge floating gin-palace shipped home by his employer at the end of his term. When his office inquired what had to be shipped back with him, he told them: "Only the usual furniture, personal effects, and junk."

But our thirty-foot, fiberglass sloop, built by Hurley in Britain, was a real yacht which we raced with mixed success among the hot local competition. It also took us on wonderful, although sometimes adventurous, cruises up the coast of the New Territories, to little islands where the *gweilos* seldom go. There, dirty little fly-blown village restaurants fed us with huge platters of crab and shrimp and fish for about two dollars a head, including a big bottle of beer.

We sailed a few times right to the gloomy, mountainous coast of Mainland China, an easy two- or three-day voyage, until the Communist gunboats turned us back. We fled, our big yellow and black spinnaker billowing among the tattered red sails of the slow, paint-bare fishing junks while the gunboats' crewmen waved their fists at our sleek little ship.

We did much entertaining in our big home. Every embassy in Hong Kong had its national day to which we were invited and which created a social debt. The Communist Chinese cadres of the New China News Agency provided many talkative lunches which had to be returned. The political advisers and government China watchers talked most freely over dinner, and wine and cognac were cheap in the colony. Other correspondents, visiting from Tokyo or Bangkok, or hit-and-run men from the home office, had to be entertained. When at home, a correspondent's job is half diplomacy, a quarter administration, and a quarter real writing work.

In order to do the diplomatic bit with some style, Marie ordered a huge rosewood dining-room table soon after we arrived in Hong Kong. We watched its progress as it was being made in a tiny, busy factory on the outskirts of Kowloon, marveling at the skill of the carver. He earned the equivalent of us$120 a month and was therefore comparatively rich, but his twelve-year-old apprentice was paid nothing except a few bowls of rice a day.

The table accommodated ten for dinner and it looked magnificent under one of the big old chandeliers. It was Marie's pride and joy until the night it collapsed.

We had decided to repay many of our social debts with one big buffet dinner for about fifty people. The table was loaded with endless varieties of great Cantonese food, cooked in our kitchen by Chinese caterers and kept warm on the table in huge bowls with flames under them.

Our maids had enlisted the aid of four of their friends to help serve the drinks and the conversation was rolling nicely when the Japanese wife of a Canadian diplomat led the way to the table. She had just picked up the first morsel in her chopsticks when the table broke slowly in the middle. The Japanese lady bent gracefully in her kimono, following the food down to the floor. She looked a little surprised and was wondering, perhaps, what a diplomat's wife should do in the unusual circumstances. She solved the problem by squatting on the floor, Japanese style, and continued to serve herself, as if tables always collapsed miraculously at correspondents' dinners so that Japanese ladies could eat in their traditional way.

But the fires from the heating bowls were burning out of control around her and the food was slithering in all directions. She was pushed gently away by running Chinese cooks who put out the fires, looking highly embarrassed.

The very diplomatic guests moved in other tables from my office and the kitchen and we continued the party which developed, people say, into one of the more lively and certainly most informal of the year's social events.

But the table collapse, which became infamous among Hong Kong's correspondents, continued to cause me trouble for months. The Chinese caterer decided we had lost face and he refused to send me a bill. I wrote him six letters explaining that it wasn't his table and nothing was his fault. But somehow he had lost much face, too, and he refused to charge anything for this disgrace, even though the amount was considerable.

My pleas for the bill were not based entirely on decency and fairness. I was stuck with a hefty separate bill for liquor and wine, which the *Star's* accountants in Toronto wouldn't approve without some official indication that it was used for a diplomatic dinner, and not for a year's personal supply or a big booze-up for the boys. I even explained this to the Chinese caterer but still he wouldn't send a bill. In the end he just ignored my letters altogether.

Eventually the bar bill was approved after I sent copies of the correspondence. But word of the night the Cahills' table collapsed spread quickly through the colony. Forever after, about half the guests we entertained seemed to surreptitiously press their elbows in testing motions when they sat down to dinner at Marie's magnificent table.

The Foreign Correspondents' Club was our main centre of relaxation. There, on the fifteenth floor of Sutherland House, adjacent to the more prestigious Hong Kong Club, you could order a dozen Australian oysters and a great New York steak for about five dollars with the wine included. Usually you could charge it to expenses, and from your table you could watch the cricket match on the green in front of the Bank of China far below.

The view from the men's washroom, over the bustling harbour with its junks down from Canton bucking the tide past the battleships of the us Seventh Fleet at anchor, was even better—the best stand-up view, the club boasted, from any urinals in the world.

But mainly the club was the meeting place for old bush-jacketed friends from the wars, with their stories and gossip and predictions, and more importantly their warnings and advice.

"If you're going to the Cambodia border use driver number five at the Oriental Hotel in Bangkok. Name's Mike. Smart old bugger knows where the bandits hit along the road and the refugees with the best stories when you get there . . . ."

"I hear you're going to Rhodesia, Jack. I just came over to tell you not to let them rent you a Volkswagen. When you go up to the border, the roads are mined and you've got to follow a big truck right in its tracks so it hits the mines first. A Beetle won't fit. Get a big car. Take care."

"No way you'll get anything out of Bangladesh by phone or wire. Just stand in the lobby of the Intercontinental and ask somebody heading for the airport to pigeon stuff out for you. Take care."

"Take care, old buddy." "Take care, cobber." "Take care, old chap." In a dozen accents it was the casual parting phrase of the correspondent, and it came from the hearts of colleagues who had earned the right to use it.

Old Richard Hughes, the London *Sunday Times* man and model for the character "Old Craw" in John Le Carré's book *The Honorable Schoolboy*, presided with great dignity and a perpetual glass of white wine over this remarkable gathering place. As the dean of the corps of correspondents, we respected him as "Your Eminence" and when we returned from a story he would acknowledge either our success, or just our safe return, with a slow sign-of-the-Cross blessing.

When I first arrived in Hong Kong, His Eminence, the be-monacled old pro from the wars in China, Japan, Korea, and wherever, greeted me with a blessing and "Welcome, Monsignor."

At a small dinner the night before I left, he patted my shoulder and said, "Goodbye, your Grace. Take care."

It was the most satisfying promotion of my life.

The Night the Brothel Burned

THERE ARE SOME GREAT HOTELS IN ASIA. The old Repulse Bay Hotel in Hong Kong (recently demolished) was one of them, with its huge rooms and antique furniture, its running room boys, and the marks of Japanese bullets from the World War II invasion still on some of the thick cement walls.

While we were looking for a permanent home and office on the island, my family and I lived for four months at the Repulse Bay. We had two rooms, paneled in rich wood, with ceilings about fifteen feet high. We overlooked the long, pure white beach, with its constant crowd of ice cream and hot dog devouring Hong Kong Chinese, who seemed desperate, for some reason I have never understood, to tan themselves.

Beyond the beach the fleets of local fishing junks spread their nets and the old, unpainted junks, down from Canton or other parts of the Communist mainland, sometimes passed by. Their crews strained at long oars when the wind was still but usually their patched and faded red sails billowed in a breeze.

The balcony of the Repulse Bay was one of the world's best places to eat and the setting among the world's most exotic. But even the best French food becomes a bit boring after a few months, so that we came to prefer the simpler meals of the coffee shop or the steaks barbecued on the hotel's broad lawns in the balmy evenings.

Raffles in Singapore, once the rambling, white second home of the British planters, is a little rundown now, with an occasional cockroach and furniture that is old without being antique. It is still a nice place to stay if you can manage to ignore the lines of tourists who gawk at you, clutching their complimentary Singapore Slings, as you dine in the magnificent dusk of the open-air Palm Court, with its starched linen and candelabra, green lawn and waving palms.

My favourite is the old section of the Oriental Hotel in Bangkok, where the two-storey rooms—comfortable living area below and bedroom above—overlook the muddy river. One can watch a stream of sampans, loaded with fruit and flowers, dead pigs and people; the long, narrow, motorized ferries, low in the water with workers and tourists; and at night the twinkling lights and cooking fires of the adventurous city.

The Taj Mahal in Bombay is magnificently ornate and efficient, its foyer constantly crowded with the rich of the poor land and their beautiful ladies in flowing saris. The new Sheraton in the same city is perhaps even more luxurious in a more modern way. You can see, from the plush comfort of your suite, hordes of ordinary Indians in a shanty town almost directly below, sleeping in the heat under slanting scraps of galvanized iron, making their homes in packing cases, gathering in big families around a cooking fire with small bowls of rice, their meal for the day. As you sip your Scotch you can see the women carrying on their heads the pitchers of water from some dirty well and you can ponder the plight of these people, who live on less in a year than you have to pay for a night at the hotel.

Hotels like these help the foreign correspondent. In the back of his mind he knows he can usually escape to one of them, often to dine in considerable style, in some places with a bottle of reasonable wine, while he contemplates what he will write about those real people in that other world he works in. This ability to escape sometimes gives him a troubled conscience. But in a strange way the blatant contrast can also encourage his sympathies and enforce his objectivity. At least he realizes that he is a very fortunate fellow indeed.

However, not all hotels in Asia are oases of riches and luxury in a desert of poverty and underprivilege. The Majestic Hotel, for instance, in Can Tho in the Mekong Delta of Vietnam, is different.

Photographer Boris Spremo and I checked into the Majestic one evening in 1973, partly because we had been told it was to become the headquarters for the Canadian forces assigned to the ICCS (International Commission of Control and Supervision) peacekeeping force in that area, and partly because it seemed to be the only hotel in town.

We were tired. We had tried to sleep the previous night in an abandoned barracks at Saigon's Tan Son Nhut airport. This was because the Vietnamese, for some reason, would not let us near the area of the airport where the Canadian peacekeeping forces were setting up their main headquarters. They had arrested a Canadian photographer and thrown him in jail. We were smuggled into the airport on the floor of an ICCS car and hid in the abandoned barracks so that we could catch the chopper to Can Tho in the morning.

The barracks was full of mosquitoes and the few thrown-away mattresses in it were full of fleas so we didn't sleep, except for a few minutes on the flight. We were told when we landed that the chopper had run through a few rounds of ground fire as we slept.

At the Can Tho air base we had picked up a jeep with a Vietnamese driver who spoke fairly good English and we spent most of the day at another airport on the outskirts of the town trying to interview a group of about a hundred female Viet Cong soldiers. The women were squatting glumly in their black pyjama suits under conical hats on the hot tarmac, waiting to be flown to North Vietnam in the first stage of a prisoner exchange.

At first the American officers wouldn't let us near them but after hours of negotiation they allowed us to interview a Canadian captain who was in charge of policing the exchange. He agreed to turn his back while we talked to the women through the driver-interpreter, providing Spremo took no pictures.

All the women would do was snarl at us. Some of them spat. None of them would say a word. But Spremo managed to shoot a few pictures from the hip, the first Western pictures of the prisoner exchange and the first in many years of Viet Cong women soldiers.

When we asked the driver what they had said when he approached them he looked embarrassed and said it wouldn't exactly translate. But when we asked him to try anyway, he told us, "They said I was a running dog of the

Yankee, imperialist bastards. You were the shit of the earth and we should all fuck off.

"I've never met any Viet Cong women before," he said with a note of distress in his voice. "They are not very nice."

The driver, who chewed constantly on a dead grasshopper, as many Mekong Delta men do for some narcotic reason, eventually drove us between the open sewers that line the highway to the town. On its outskirts, not far from the American base, he pointed to a ramshackle shack bearing a big sign in English proclaiming "The Happy Fuck."

"Number one bar that," he said, chewing on his grasshopper. "Hell of a good place. Not very pricey."

When we got to the Majestic Hotel, a four- or five-storey building across the dusty main road from the Mekong River, he described it similarly and, we should have realized, ominously. "Number one place," he said. "Not very pricey. Lots of fun place."

When Spremo and I checked in we were given the numbers of rooms on the second floor, but no keys. And when I began to open the door to my room a shrill voice shouted something in Vietnamese, which sounded similar to the remarks of the Viet Cong women at the airport.

While I was contemplating this situation, Spremo emerged from his room across the corridor clutching his nose and looking strangely pale.

"I try to go to the bathroom," he said in the thick Yugoslav accent he hadn't lost in two decades in Canada. "I open the door and the smell knocks me over. So I slam the smell in so it can't get out. I think there is something dead in the bathroom. Do you have a bathroom?"

"I don't know yet," I told him. "There's somebody in my room."

We went to the clerk on the first floor who had booked us in and told him there was something dead in Boris' bathroom and somebody alive in my room. He shrugged and told us to wait a while and he'd fix it up. Then after about five minutes he told us to go back to our rooms. Now mine was empty except for two cockroaches as big as frogs in the corner. They were too big to stomp on because of the mess they would have made. And there was a rat running around inside the glass lampshade. It made the already dim light come in oddly varying intensities as it moved around the bulb.

There was a small, low bed in the room with a dirty cover and that was all, except for a door with peeling paint leading to a bathroom. I opened it with great care. There was a hole in the bare and filthy cement floor for a toilet and a rusty pipe in a corner with a shower attachment.

A woman knocked at the door of my room while I was surveying the bathroom and asked if I wanted her to stay. She was very fat and she didn't seem to have any teeth. She got quite upset when I told her to go away. Spremo was upset too when he knocked. He looked even paler than before.

"I open the door again just a little bit," he said. "And the stench you wouldn't believe. There is something dead in there, maybe some*body*. I not open the door again. Do you have a bathroom?"

Boris used the bathroom and emerged looking a little better. "You cheated," he accused me. "You took the room with the good bathroom."

"Boris," I said, "I have become convinced that, in general, this is not one of the better hotels." I showed him the rat in the lampshade.

The food in the restaurant on the ground floor wasn't very good either, mainly rice with a shrimp or two in it.

While we were eating the kitchen exploded and the building caught fire. Jets of fire spurted suddenly toward our table, as if from a flame thrower. The kitchen was a yelling mess of brown men and burning fat. We ran into the street.

Spremo can be an excitable fellow especially if anything occurs that might stop him doing his job. The first thing he thought of, maybe the only thing, was his precious collection of cameras hidden under the bed in his room.

He ran through the hotel's main entrance up the staircase and, although it was the opposite of common sense, I followed him. The stairs were on fire and we were scorched a bit as we ran down them, clutching cameras, typewriter and notebooks. Then we stood in the street and watched the arrival of a fire brigade consisting of scores of shrilly vocal men towing galvanized tanks of water on hand carts.

There is something funny about a burning brothel. Maybe there shouldn't be, but there is. It is not the *déshabille* of the emerging clientele, but the expressions on their faces. There is a strange mixture of shock and shame, combined with false attempts at casual unconcern and complete detachment, probably unseen on the human face except in these circmstances. There is also no gallantry in a burning brothel. The men, all of them Vietnamese or Chinese—because the Majestic was obviously an institution for wealthier locals—charged first down the burning stairs, pulling up pants and pushing the girls aside. The towels some of them had wrapped around their bodies were ripped away and they were running around with only two hands and three or four places to put them.

Despite their primitive equipment, the yelling fire brigade managed somehow to confine the fire to the restaurant, staircase and part of the first floor of the hotel, and put it out after an hour or so. So Spremo and I were able to return to our rooms to sleep. But Boris never did open his bathroom door again. And I tried not to disturb the rat and the cockroaches. Twice during the night I managed to be polite in rejecting disheveled ladies who seemed to be going for fire-sale prices.

There are many great hotels in Asia and the image of the foreign correspondent living the luxurious life, even covering the wars from the comfort of his suite, is sometimes justified. But the Majestic in Can Tho is not one of these hotels. And unfortunately on some jobs there are just as many Majestics as there are Taj Mahals.

In the long run, to save expenses, I learned to dispense with Spremo and his photographer colleagues and to take my own pictures, which was a mistake. It is risky to travel alone anywhere in the world. In the troubled areas where the stories are it is stupid. It is also impossible to observe an occurrence properly through the lens of a Nikon. You either focus on one point and miss the overall picture or you stand back and observe a situation objectively and fully, and miss the picture on film.

In a war situation the photographer has to take many more risks than the writer. He has to walk those extra ten yards or so into the minefield to get the best angle, or stand upright in the ditch to get his shot. Those extra ten yards make the difference and they take guts. To do his work the photographer has to stay and face the problem while the writer is running away from artillery shells or a mob. The cameramen, TV and still, are the journalistic heroes of the wars.

But throughout the period of covering the Canadian ICCS corps in Vietnam, the ebullient, excitable, handsome

Spremo, winner of more than 150 awards and one of the world's best hard-news photographers, was with me. He'd be raring to get where the action was, hustling to get back to Saigon to wire his pictures through the Associated Press (AP) or United Press International (UPI) wire services, or fretting at my insistence that I had to talk to people or go somewhere where there would be no picture. He threw some of the best parties in Saigon for his photographer friends—except the one time he bought his Scotch on the black market and served his guests with pure urine.

Shortly before the experience at the Majestic we had flown up to Hue, the ancient spiritual capital of Vietnam, along with John Walker, of Southam News Service, to cover the Canadians setting up their headquarters for peacekeeping in the northern areas. They were establishing themselves in an old hotel on the banks of the Perfume River. Two officers who had been sent to operate an outpost in the bombed-out city of Quang Tri, on the border between North and South Vietnam, had been unable to reach the city. They had met with heavy artillery fire on the way and been forced to turn back.

Walker, Spremo, and I, along with an NBC TV crew from Chicago, who were in the area ahead of us, decided, over a huge meal of crab and beer at the Canadian headquarters, that it would be a good story if we went in where the peacekeepers didn't dare go. In so doing, we thought, we could illustrate the difficulties of peacekeeping in a war that wasn't over, although everybody in North America appeared to have swallowed the Kissinger-Nixon line that there was not only peace in Vietnam but also honour.

The NBC men made a deal. They had a letter of introduction to a South Vietnamese general at a headquarters
near Quang Tri, who might allow us into the city. We had a
Canadian flag which might be recognized as a symbol of
neutrality and stop somebody shooting at us. We'd be the
NBC crew as far as the general was concerned. They'd be
Canadians if any shooting started.

We rented two white-painted jeeps and their drivers,
who bargained expensively for them in advance and de-
pleted the cash supply of our Canadian group to almost
nothing. But the drivers assured us the banks would be
open on our return to Hue and would take travellers'
cheques, so we could then purchase Air Vietnam tickets to
get back to Saigon to file our stories.

We set out in a two-jeep convoy, with the Canadian
flag flying from our leading vehicle, across the bombed-
down and patched-together bridges on the road to Quang
Tri, about sixty miles away. In the little villages of huts
made from ammunition crates and shell casings, the main
economic activity seemed to be coffin making. Every village had three or four coffin shops.

Soldiers stopped us at checkpoints along the way,
wondered about the white and red maple leaf flag and let
us through after we explained we were *bo chi* (journalists)
from a neutral, peacekeeping country. Some of them
seemed to know where Canada was, but they thought it
was a part of the US. We had to explain the peace treaty and
the role of the ICCS to them.

The village where the general had his headquarters
was off the main highway not far from Quang Tri. The NBC
letter of introduction worked. The general gave us a note
instructing his men in the city to look after us. But he also
warned us not to go.

A shell exploded in a deep ditch, about a hundred

yards behind our jeeps, as we turned onto the main high-way again, sending a column of water high in the air. A heavy artillery barrage hit along the roadside as we ap-proached the city.

Quang Tri, once the home of over 60,000 people, was in fact not a city. It was a horrible mess of rubble, a collec-tion of huge pockmarks from the bombs of B-52s. It looked like the surface of the moon, with nothing standing higher than a few feet, except one little bombed-out building. The only inhabitants were four Vietnamese soldiers and a cap-tain in faded battle dress in an obvious state of fatigue in this one predominant pile of rubble which used to be the city's hospital.

We could see a South Vietnamese flag flying at the edge of where the city had been and beyond that, across the river, a Viet Cong flag. And to the east, half a mile away, the artillery barrage was hitting, about a shell a min-ute, in approximately the same place, sending up columns of black smoke and making much noise.

Spremo wanted a picture of the two flags with the ar-tillery barrage in the background. So did the NBC crew. But the Vietnamese captain said we couldn't go closer because the whole area was mined and two of his men had been killed the previous day. But it was too much for the NBC crew. They knew what their zoom lens could do with the artillery barrage—even though it was so far away—and the two flags in the background while the correspondent did his stand-up stuff. They'd get maybe thirty seconds of air time, despite the fact that Vietnam was not making the tube at home at all any more. And Spremo knew what his long-distance lenses could do, providing he got the right angle.

So eventually the captain, who wore a very tired smile, said we could go as long as we walked exactly in the footsteps of a soldier he would send to lead the way through the minefield. And he stressed that he meant that exactly, by making us practice in the safe dirt near his rubble headquarters, stepping single file in the footsteps of the man in front.

It occurred to me during the practice that there was no need for me to go at all because I could see all that was happening perfectly well for my purposes from where I was. In fact, it seemed eminently commonsensical not to go.

"Hey Boris," I said casually. "There's really no need for John and I to go. We can see it all from here."

Spremo didn't say anything. Neither did Walker, the NBC crew, nor the Vietnamese captain. There was just a silence. So I said, "OK, I'm coming," and we went, picking our way painstakingly in the short footsteps of the little soldier. Spremo, looking through the lens of his Nikon at the smoke from the artillery barrage, began to wander away off course, so I had to run after him, swearing at him, to pull him back into the line.

We could see the Viet Cong soldiers in their black battle dress on the other side of the river and we waved to them, but they just stared back with puzzled expressions. The artillery barrage intensified cooperatively just as the NBC man was doing his thing in front of the camera. The sound man muttered gleefully, "Good bang bangs, great bang bangs." Spremo got some good pictures.

Perhaps it was because most of us were looking at it through long-distance lenses, but the barrage seemed to be coming closer so we picked our way more hurriedly back through the minefield to the jeeps. It was noon now and the plane to Saigon, the only place from where we could wire the film and file our stories, left Hue at 2:30 p.m. It was already midnight in Toronto, only six hours before the morning deadline. But lots of time, really, even though we had to stop at the bank in Hue to get some money to pay our fares.

The NBC crew sped away and we didn't see them again. They were to stay in Hue to do some more stories. They could ship their film on the plane and have it picked up in Saigon. The TV crews always had good logistical backups, but newspaper people rarely did, except perhaps those from *The New York Times* and one or two other major newspapers with staffs in Saigon. We had to carry our own stuff.

We were tired by now. Walking across minefields is an emotional drain. The noise of the artillery barrage had been wearying, even though it never came really close to us. And as we passed through one of the little coffin villages the front wheels of the jeep began to wobble violently. The driver pulled to the side of the road looking sheepish.

Spremo didn't like this sort of thing to happen when he had undeveloped film of consquence in his camera. He became excited. He jumped from the jeep and began kicking the wheels and ordering the driver to drive on anyway. The driver produced a big hammer from the back of the jeep, and for a while I thought he was going to hit Spremo with it. But instead he hit the jeep wheels hard and many times, then finally agreed we should drive slowly on. We had wasted about half an hour.

When we got to the bank at Hue on the wobbly wheels it was after 1:30 p.m. and the bank was closed until 3:00 p.m. for a siesta period the driver had forgotten to warn us about. This made Spremo angry again, but he calmed down when I said we'd ask the Canadian ICCS team, in the headquarters across the river, to lend us the money for our air fares.

On the way, halfway across the bridge, the jeep finally

gave up altogether. One of the wheels fell off. Spremo tried to put it back on, covering his bush jacket with grease in the process, but it didn't work. The driver promised he'd find another jeep somewhere. In the meantime we ran about a mile in the hundred-degree heat to the ICCS headquarters.

When we had stopped puffing and sweating enough to make sense of ourselves, the captain in charge said fine, he'd lend us the money, but all of the cash in the post's possession was, for some reason he never explained, in a car on the way to the airport. If we could find the car, he said, we should tell the sergeant it was OK to take what we needed as long as we gave him a receipt.

In the meantime our driver had turned up at the headquarters in a new jeep, but its wheels, too, began to wobble almost uncontrollably on the way to the airport. We never found the ICCS car with the money.

The Air Vietnam Boeing 707 was already boarding when we arrived and the tumbledown terminal was packed with a babbling horde, clutching string bags and baskets and clamouring for the few spare seats still apparently available.

Spremo became excited again. He spoke in English to a pretty girl in a yellow *ao dai* who was selling the tickets, stating what must have been obvious—he had about six cameras hanging from his neck—that he was a photographer who had to get to Saigon in a hurry and that we would all pay our fares by cheque now or by cash after we got to Saigon. She smiled at him.

He tried it again in primitive French, in a somewhat higher pitch, and the girl began to look puzzled. Then he began shouting at her in Yugoslavian, pounding the ticket counter. She began to look distressed.

There was one other European in the terminal who

looked as if he might be a journalist so I introduced myself. He was a nice young man from the Knight newspapers
in the States and he emptied his wallet of piastres so that
we were able to scrape up just enough between us all to
buy our tickets.

Walker and I wrote our stories during the two-hour
flight and we arrived at Tan Son Nhut airport with several
hours to spare before my morning Toronto deadline. But
the long drive to downtown Saigon in the afternoon rush
hour was never easy and this time it was worse than usual.
The streets were packed with screaming Hondas, carrying
anything from two to five people. Bullock carts blocked
several intersections and army trucks crawled ahead of us.
A crooked cop (assuming there were any who weren't
crooked) pulled us aside near the big Buddhist temple and
bargained with the driver for more than half an hour before
he was able to elicit enough bribe money to allow us to
proceed.

There was only one way to file a story quickly out of
Saigon in those days. The wire services, especially Reuters
which I always used, did their best, but there was invariably a pile of stories in their baskets at this time of day. One
was expected to ask for priority over colleagues only in
highly exceptional circumstances. The only quick way was
through a single telephone booth in an old building kitty-
corner from the Caravelle Hotel on Tu Do Street. From
here, after bribing the clerk in charge of phone calls, you
could get a direct line to Oakland, California, and be
switched through to Canada.

You had to close the door to this tiny phone booth to
deaden the noise of the Hondas outside. Then no air could
get in and it was the hottest place on earth. There was nowhere to put your notes as you dictated a story, so the combination of oozing sweat from your hands and big drips

29

from your face made your notes soggy and unreadable. I have seen reporters come from this phone booth, remove their bush jackets, and wring them out like wet towels. And this particular day was a hot one. What sweat I had left after the mile run in Hue poured out onto my notes.

When I got through to the foreign desk in Toronto, a young editor who had just come on shift was grumpy.

"I wish you'd learn to file earlier, Jack," he said. "It's only an hour before deadline. It's a hell of a busy day. And I had a tough time getting to work in the traffic this morning."

I was too tired and sweaty to argue.

"Will you just get me a copytaker?" I said.

IIII

The Switched-Off War

WHEN HENRY KISSINGER, the US presidential adviser, won a Nobel Peace Prize for bringing a settlement to Vietnam, the American people, and others throughout the Western world, tended to take the award seriously.

There was a widespread belief abroad that the hyperactive and unusual diplomat had indeed organized something remarkable in his long negotiations with North Vietnamese emissary Le Duc Tho in Paris throughout 1972, and at the final peace talks in Paris in January, 1973. People wanted to believe that Kissinger had put an end to the war that had killed more than four million men, including over 58,000 Americans, and had created a crisis of conscience for almost twelve years in the United States.

In particular, the men in the executive offices of the TV networks in New York believed the claims by Kissinger and President Richard Nixon that they had at last achieved "peace with honour" in Vietnam. This was partly because, like most other good Americans, they desperately wanted to believe it, partly because the war coverage was expensive, and also because, with the final withdrawal of American troops in 1973, stories from the area would be without American content and therefore without much news value.

There's no story, someone said, in gooks killing gooks.

In Vietnam, though, the war went on. About ten thousand Vietnamese continued to die every month in the slaughter. Families still wept at the big cemetery in Bien Hua outside Saigon where the dead soldiers were buried. In the village of An My, twenty-five miles north of Saigon, Mrs. Phan Thi-Xinh, an elderly widow, woke up in the early hours of the morning of January 28, 1973—the official date of the ceasefire—to find eight dead soldiers in the patch of banana trees behind her home. Later that day her little stone house was destroyed in an artillery attack. She didn't believe me when I told her the Americans said the war was over.

In Ottawa, Canadian External Affairs Minister Mitchell Sharp was almost as skeptical as Mrs. Xinh. He was startled when he received a phone call from us Secretary of State William Rogers announcing, just before the peace pact was concluded, that Canada had been nominated to the four-member International Commission of Control and Supervision (iccs) to police the peace.

Neither Sharp, Prime Minister Pierre Trudeau, nor any other Canadian official, had ever been consulted about possible Canadian participation in the peacekeeping force. Sharp, a normally calm, phlegmatic man, gasped at the presumption of his American counterpart and at the blatant intrusion into Canadian affairs.

But Rogers persisted. Negotiations in Paris were delicate, he said. If Canada pulled out it would ruin the agreement. Surely Canada wouldn't want to do anything to ruin the chances of peace in Vietnam.

"We were put in a terrible spot," Sharp told me later, after he'd ended a distinguished political career. "We were, of course, very interested in peace in Vietnam, but it was our opinion that the terms of the treaty were unrealistic and that there was, in fact, no peace in Vietnam. We were in effect being committed by the Americans to send Canadian troops into a situation in which many of them could be killed."

A few days later, on a Sunday morning, a group of eight Canadian external affairs officials sat at the long table in the "operations room" in the East Block of Ottawa's Parliament Buildings and played a deadly serious game.

Some of them pretended they were Hungarians while others played the roles of Poles or Indonesians, the other three nationalities which were "invited" to participate, along with Canada, in the proposed peacekeeping force. All of them, from time to time, switched back to playing the part of Canadians in the force. This was an easy role because most of them had had long, often frustrating, personal experience in Southeast Asia with the ineffective Internal Control Commission (ICC) formed under the Geneva agreement of 1954 to report on outbreaks of hostilities in Indochina. Poland and India were the other ICC members.

These eight men, joined at times by other top external affairs and defence department officials, argued, pleaded and tried out all of their diplomatic tricks for more than sixteen hours without a break, until about three the following morning, when they were all exhausted.

They reached the basic conclusion that the peacekeeping operation proposed by Kissinger at the Paris peace talks, and pushed on Canada by Secretary of State Rogers, would not work.

Worse, these weary men decided, Canada could be trapped as a scapegoat, blamed for the naiveté of Kissinger and Nixon, if it participated in a peacekeeping operation which was certain to fail. At the same time, however, they drew up a rigid set of rules, based on Canada's eighteen years of experience in Vietnam with the ICC, which might make peacekeeping practicable, if rigidly applied.

Sharp then unleashed a flurry of diplomatic activity around the world that confirmed the gloomy judgment of the eight men in the "operations room." Nick Etheridge, Canada's man in Hanoi, tried to consult with the North Vietnamese government but was only able to contact some minor officials. Subsequently David Jackson, Canada's senior representative in Saigon flew into Hanoi on an ICC aircraft and received assurance from high officials in the foreign ministry that Canada would be acceptable as one of the peacekeeping participants. But when he mentioned Canada's conditions he was told: "Let's have peace first, then we can discuss details."

He was also told that North Vietnam envisaged a peacekeeping force of about 250 men compared with the 1,500 contemplated by the Americans.

John Halstead, then assistant under-secretary of state for external affairs, flew to Warsaw and Budapest for talks with the Poles and Hungarians. The Poles indicated they understood Canada's concerns in light of their common experience as members of the ICC, but the Hungarians suggested it should be an honour to serve on such a commission and said they didn't want to get bogged down with details. And from Indonesia, the other nonCommunist member, Ambassador Tom Delworth, an old Indochina hand, reported that there would be many complexities.

Still, Sharp was stuck with the American warning that if Canada rejected a role in the force there might be no peace treaty. He agreed that Canada would participate for sixty days, providing the conditions laid down by the eight men in the "operations room" game were met. "I don't know if the Americans tried to negotiate the conditions or not," Sharp said later. "But we didn't get most of them."

Frustrated and disgusted, bitterly opposed by many of his own officials, a full 45 per cent of whom had cut their diplomatic teeth in Southeast Asia, Sharp pushed approval for participation through Parliament. And because the key condition—that a "continuing political authority" like the United Nations Security Council, would assume responsibility for the peace settlement and receive reports from the commission or any of its members—was not achieved, he proclaimed a unilateral "open mouth policy." This meant that Canada would say what it liked, through the press or any vehicle available, and thus, in effect, report directly to the free world.

The "open mouth" policy made coverage of the ICCS activities in Vietnam a ball. Sharp appointed Michel Gauvin, the Canadian ambassador to Greece, to take charge of the peacekeeping operation from Saigon. He talked his head off to the press, to the Americans, to the North Vietnamese, and the Viet Cong, and he told everybody else what he had told the others and what they had told him. Within his first week in Saigon he was nicknamed "Open Mouth" Gauvin.

The *Star's* Mark Gayn wrote: "If Michel Gauvin didn't exist we would have had to invent him for the peace-keeper's job in South Vietnam. Indeed, it is difficult to think of another person who could have done as well in the face of such handicaps of human hostility, twisted politics and unkind nature."

Gleefully, Gauvin blasted off in an oddly undiplomatic way at the Poles, the Hungarians, the Americans, or anybody else whenever he felt the urge. He created embarrassment almost everywhere, and huge amounts of respect and gratitude amongst the members of the small press corps covering the ICCS activities.

And Gauvin was only the leader of the "open mouths." Even corporals among Canada's 290-man peace force held forth to the press or anybody who wanted to listen to their views. They discussed world affairs, the progress of the alleged peace, the stupidities of their colleagues from the Communist countries, their disgust with American bureaucracy, and anything else they wanted to say as citizens of a free country that believed in free speech—even for unfortunates in the army.

I was shuttling between Saigon and Ottawa at this stage of the story. In Ottawa the press spokesman for the department of external affairs, Dick Gorham, another old Southeast Asia hand, was out-blabbing even the great Open Mouth Gauvin. At one background briefing in the Parliament Buildings he criticized us for not asking the right questions. Then he told us that the right questions to ask concerned Canadian-American relations. "And if you want to know the answers," he added, "I just happen to have some highly-confidential documents I'll leave on the desk here in case anybody wants to take a surreptitious peek on the way out."

In Vietnam, because of the American commitment of Canada to the cause, Canadian servicemen and diplomats were shot at, their helicopters were the targets of heat-seeking SAM missiles, their peacekeeping outposts umbrella'd by artillery barrages, and the roads they travelled heavily mined. Fortunately only one Canadian was killed, when a SAM hit a helicopter, and two were held as captives by the Viet Cong as alleged US spies, before Sharp and the Canadian government pulled out the "peacekeepers" after a sixty-day extension of the original sixty-day term.

In the circumstances, early in 1973, there was some Canadian newspaper space and airtime for the war, but very little anywhere else in the world. The Canadian interest also evaporated rapidly as soon as the "peacekeepers" were called home. The American people continued to heave their great sigh of relief that the war was over, and the TV executives in New York continued to do nothing to convince them otherwise. The foreign correspondents drank or grumbled their frustrations away in the clubs of Hong Kong, Bangkok, and Tokyo. And the Vietnamese continued to destroy each other in enormous ugly numbers.

Peter Hively, the Asian bureau chief for the American Broadcasting Company, came to our home in Hong Kong for dinner one evening in mid 1973. He announced, with a dazed look on his face, that his office had ordered him to go to Saigon to close down the network's bureau there.

"But the war's not over," I said. "Did you tell them the war isn't over?"

"I told them maybe a dozen times," Hively said. "But they said we have peace with honour in Vietnam and there's nothing happening there. They said Kissinger says the war is over. Nixon says the war is over. So the war's over. And when I insisted the war wasn't over they treated me as if I was some sort of nut. They just wouldn't believe me."

In the end, Hively said, he thought the only way he could convince the bureaucrats in the head office that the war still waged was to insist on combat pay, a small supplement paid to some US correspondents in war zones, before he'd go to Saigon to close the bureau. But even that didn't work.

"They told me that was OK," he said. "They said I could have combat pay to go to Vietnam to close the bureau because the war was over. They just don't want to believe us. They don't like the war so they've switched the damn thing off," he said.

Hively's aircraft had to swerve to avoid a few artillery fights before it landed in Saigon, but he closed the bureau and he collected his combat pay.

Through 1973, 1974, up to the early spring of 1975, the world's great apathy towards the wars in Indochina continued unabated. The correspondents were called home or they found their stories elsewhere, watching, mostly from Hong Kong or Tokyo, the beginning of the demise of Chairman Mao Zedong in China, the struggle of Japan to continue the economic miracle, and the increasing megalomania of India's prime minister, Indira Gandhi.

Among the eighty or so correspondents based in Hong Kong, only a few, mostly magazine writers, were allowed to take any direct interest in the events in Vietnam and they were on long-term projects with vague, unurgent deadlines.

Tony Paul, the huge, able Australian roving editor for *Reader's Digest*, occasionally brought firsthand news of the war back to the rest of us at the Foreign Correspondents' Club and we could understand from the wires the frustrations of the few correspondents still in Saigon. But still there was no interest at home.

Paul's editors had asked him to research and write a piece for the US editions entitled "Can South Vietnam Survive the Peace?" But the events caught up with the idea, and eventually with Paul himself, before the article could be published.

Paul flew to Saigon in November, 1974, to interview US Ambassador Graham Martin, who told him: "About ten

years from now, South Vietnam will be a rich little capitalist country with a minor problem of Communist terrorism in its remoter border provinces—really nothing
more than banditry, the sort of problem that many other
Asian nations have to contend with.''

Then Paul had trouble arranging his most important interview—until he was suddenly advised in Hong Kong that
the president, Nguyen Van Thieu, would receive him at his
palace in Saigon on Saturday, March 8, 1975.

Uncomfortable in an unaccustomed business suit and
itching in the heat, Paul was met by the shrewd, tough, corrupt president on the patio of the palace. It was the last
interview given by Thieu as president of the Republic of
South Vietnam.

Thieu said he was deeply worried about the growing
reluctance of the us Congress to grant more aid for his
country, but nevertheless he was highly optimistic about
economic developments at home. The rice crop had never
been better, he said. American and Canadian companies
appeared to have discovered major offshore oil deposits
likely to be earning millions of dollars by 1979. Capital
would be flowing into the country as soon as businessmen
realized the advantages of South Vietnam's cheap labor and
her new laws encouraging foreign investors.

Paul asked him why he had granted the interview at
this particular time.

"Oh," said Thieu casually, "I've just finished a reor-
ganization of the civil service and I've got some spare time
on my hands."

At almost the exact moment that Thieu was expressing
his languorous optimism on his palace patio a small group
of Communist signallers were surreptitiously checking into
the Anh Dao Hotel in Ban Me Thout, three hundred miles
away in South Vietnam's central highlands. They set up

their smuggled radios on the top floors of the old hotel. At first light the next day, acting as spotters, they began to direct a massive artillery barrage against the headquarters' compound and the tank and artillery bases of the town's defenders, the Twenty-third Division of the Army of the Republic of Vietnam (ARVN).

The men on the hotel roof also signalled the start of the end of the war. Within two days Ban Me Thout had fallen, threatening the security of the two larger central highlands towns of Pleiku and Kontum. Within a week Thieu had ordered a disastrous retreat from all of the highlands. Just fifty-three days after Thieu's optimistic interview on the palace patio, the North Vietnamese tanks rolled across the palace lawns and men from the jungles, wearing pith helmets, were patrolling the palace balconies, gaping at the unknown wonders of a city as they strolled Tu Do Street. They complained to the staff of the Caravelle Hotel that when they washed their rice in the toilet bowls, it disappeared down the drains of the "rice washing machines."

When the central highlands fell in mid-March of 1975, and Saigon thus seemed to be vaguely threatened, the TV executives in New York switched the war on again. The newspaper editors began to see on the screen what they hadn't wanted to believe was happening. Rooms in the correspondents' hotels, the Caravelle and the Continental Palace, opposite each other in Saigon's main city square, suddenly became scarce again. Rumuntcho's restaurant, where most of us ate most of the time, had to use its upstairs room to look after the overflow.

These were good days for a correspondent in Saigon. There were stories and excitement without much danger. Old friends arrived almost daily from all parts of the world. The food was good at Rumuntcho's, especially the cheese soufflé, and the house wine served in wooden jugs was cheap, plentiful, and respectable. Or you could dine with more class on French cuisine at the Guilliaume Tell, sit over an endless variety of Vietnamese crab dishes at the big restaurant on the riverfront, overlooking the old Saigon Yacht Club, or try, for a change, the Chinese restaurants of Cholon. During the day, if you had time, you could swim or play tennis with the rich establishment at the exclusive *Cercle Sportif.*

The same old drivers we had used in the days of the "real" war, with the same old rattletrap cars, greeted us like old friends and fought for our services, offering everything from cheaper, newer, better girls to cheaper and quicker civil servants in charge of the issuance of exit visas and curfew passes.

With the Americans gone there was a glut of girls. Many of them were semi-amateurs and still beautiful, but the ravages of war were obvious in the painted faces and sloppy bodies of the battered professionals in the dark bars along Tu Do Street. They were also desperate. They rattled embarrassingly on the bar windows as you passed, trying to encourage you inside with smiles so false and gestures so crude they'd discourage, surely, even the randiest of rapists.

But the hostesses at the rooftop bar of the Miramar Hotel were mostly new or attractive still in their colourful *ao dais* and, as ever, they could be charged as room service on the hotel bill if you were staying there.

One Scandinavian TV correspondent, who lived with his crew at the Miramar, fell seriously and genuinely in love with a beautiful, blonde secretary at one of the Scandinavian embassies, but was unable to impress her even after weeks of intense and ardent effort. Finally, on his birthday, she agreed to be entertained briefly, for a drink and a chat, in his hotel room.

But the correspondent's crew had also decided to give him a birthday present—three girls from the rooftop bar. When he entered his room with the innocent secretary on his arm, they were met by a roomful of naked ladies shouting, as instructed by the crew: "Happy Birthday! Have a fuck!"

The Scandinavian was very gloomy about his broken romance for about a week afterward, but he recovered, and eventually even made friends again with his crew.

The city was normal and the people went about their business as usual. Con Cua (The Crab)—the beggar boy with a paralysed spine—continued to crawl along Tu Do Street on all fours and the noseless leper plied his constant trade in front of the Catholic cathedral. The widows of the war begged as usual in the restaurants and the "homeless," using rented, skinny, starving kids, hustled aggressively in the streets for a few coins. The ex-soldiers with no legs thumped the pavements with their arms and stumps to attract attention.

The enormous talents of Ti Ti, the jasmine girl, had been honed to perfection by now. Ti Ti (Vietnamese for littlest one) was about six years old and knee-high to a 105-millimetre howitzer shell. If you refused her sales pitch for a string of sweet-smelling jasmine she would curse you in a shrill voice that drowned the noise of the home-going Hondas, starting with "You number-ten cheap Charlie" and ending with her opinion of your pedigree through at least three incestuous generations.

Ti Ti's turf was the Continental Palace Hotel and she lived in the jeep that belonged to the Associated Press, whose writers had more or less adopted her, and who described her in one dispatch:

In addition to limpid almond eyes and a woebegone smile of unquestionable innocence, Ti Ti had the inborn gift of the con. Her strategy was to lurk among the potted plants of the hotel's terrace bar, barefoot in her tattered dress, until a young helicopter pilot or civilian engineer entered with a girl on his arm.

"Frowers for a pletty rady," Ti Ti would intone in her fractured English, pushing a string of fragrant jasmine blossoms under the lady's nose.

If the man refused he was immediately exposed as a "cheap, cheap Charlie" or worse. The abuse grew in volume as the couple moved toward a table and abated only when Ti Ti was paid to go away.

Then when dinner was served on the terrace, Ti Ti would stare hungrily in, like a Third-World famine poster, at the diners.

And as they walked away, usually throwing her a face-saving coin or two, she would occasionally be seen standing on tippy toes to relieve the donor of his watch or ring, which she took for safekeeping to her friend Con Cua, The Crab.

Still, despite Ti Ti and her friends, Saigon was not a bad place to be. The US field observers were filing realistic reports of the war to the US Embassy where nobody seemed to take the slightest notice of them. Ambassador Graham Martin still appeared to believe that Vietnam would turn into a rich little capitalist country with a minor problem of Communist terrorism in its remoter border provinces. But the military attachés from other nations, the British, and especially the Australians, were frank with their gloomy and accurate assessments of the situation.

The TV crews and still cameramen still had to drive miles into the countryside or fly far north to get any really good bang bangs. A writing journalist did just as well by listening to their stories and talking to the military analysts in the safety of Saigon.

Despite the American optimism, it was a story, there was no doubt, of a country that was collapsing quickly, dramatically, and as the later years proved, disastrously.

IV

The Death of a City

NOBODY REALLY CARED MUCH about Cambodia. The Americans bombed the beautiful, gentle land with extraordinary ferocity from 1969 to 1973, then forgot about it. The media remembered the twenty-one men it had left dead in the jungles, or at least their fellow correspondents remembered. The readers and viewers at home couldn't care less so the bureaus either closed, cut down to a single, lonely staffer, or left it all to a local stringer until it became fairly obvious in the spring of 1975 that the capital of Phnom Penh was going to fall to the Khmer Rouge guerrillas.

Only the French, who kept their Agence France Presse correspondents fairly busy, Syd Schanberg of *The New York Times,* and Neil Davis, a young, freelance television cameraman from Tasmania, seemed to care.

Davis lived in Phnom Penh and loved it probably more than his native Australian island. With his baby face, blond curly hair, and a limp from several shrapnel wounds, he was to become the correspondents' correspondent as the Cambodian and Vietnam wars ended. In Cambodia he knew everybody and everything. Members of the Lon Nol government whispered in his ear. So did the military attachés of the embassies. The ordinary people, especially the women, seemed to have a particular affection for him. And when the hit-and-run correspondents came back toward the end he shared his information, experience, and advice freely with all of us.

It was a bit unusual, under the media snobbery system, to have a TV cameraman as the dean and chief advisor of the press corps, but Davis was an unusual man. Sensibly he escaped from his beloved Cambodia just before Phnom Penh fell. The Khmer Rouge could have had him singled out for special treatment. He remained in Saigon after that city fell, took the only TV pictures of the Viet Cong tanks rolling into the presidential palace and then he manned the Reuters wire service during the early days of the occupation, sending out some of the most important and dramatic dispatches of the thirty-year war.

Eventually NBC recognized what every correspondent knew about Davis and made him a staff correspondent based in Bangkok. When he occasionally entered the Foreign Correspondents' Club of Hong Kong, he was mobbed by old friends who loved him and by the new wave of less-experienced aspirants in Asia who regarded him with awe.

Davis and I spent a couple of nights in my hotel room in Phnom Penh, over a bottle of Scotch, while rockets crunched in the distance, discussing the history of Cambodia and trying to guess what was about to happen. Three names kept emerging in the conversation, names I'd never heard before: Khieu Samphan, Ieng Sary, and Saloth Sar, alias Pol Pot. Davis called them the phantoms of the jungle and we talked of them in terms of hope that they might become the saviours of the then-corrupt, deeply troubled land.

We were very wrong. These men, isolated in the jungle, saturated with ideology, unaffected by the small advances made by civilization during their lonely decade of struggle and hate, were to become infamous in the next few years as the architects of one of history's most horrible crimes: the mass murder of their own countrymen.

Obviously, nobody with any sense was flying into Cambodia in March, 1975, so when Tony Clifton of *Newsweek* and I booked on the Air Camboge flight from Hong Kong to Phnom Penh we were the only passengers. The rest of the Caravelle jet was occupied by crates of rice and military equipment. But it was Air Camboge's scheduled and much advertised "champagne flight," and there was enough good French champagne on board to serve a full planeload of a hundred people, with a full crew of Cambodian flight attendants to look after them. We took full advantage.

Consequently when the jet, half of the airline's fleet, swooped and swerved to avoid a rocket attack as we landed at Phnom Penh's Pontechong airport, Clifton and I weren't all that worried about it. We were even somewhat amused by the small group of correspondents who had been covering the rocket attack and who kept yelling at us, "Run, you stupid bastards," as we sauntered happily and casually across to the terminal where they were sheltering.

The only correspondent who wasn't scared in Cambodia during that time was Al Rockoff, a photographer who freelanced for the AP, and who seemed to be dressed constantly in the same old pair of jeans and dirty T-shirt. Al wasn't scared because he had already been killed.

In 1974, a few months before the fall of Phnom Penh, he was at the front taking pictures when a shell burst near him and riddled his body with shrapnel. One of the old green vans the Cambodians used as ambulances rushed him to a hospital in the capital, but by the time he arrived his heart had stopped. There are various versions of how long his heart had stopped beating, ranging from ten minutes to half an hour. Nobody will ever know because nobody in the ambulance checked during the long ride.

But as soon as he was admitted to the hospital, already crowded with wounded soldiers, a Scandinavian nurse began to pummel his chest, massage his heart and give him mouth-to-mouth resuscitation.

Almost miraculously Rockoff began to breathe again. In a few weeks he had recovered enough to be sent to Bangkok for some rest. He was back in Phnom Penh with his battery of cameras, and dressed in the same old jeans and T-shirt, a few weeks before the fall.

One morning, as the Khmer Rouge were bombarding the Pontechong airport with rockets and a few were whistling over the city itself, Rockoff joined a group of us sitting around the pool at the old Hotel Le Phnom. He remarked, after a while, "Well, I think I'll go out to the airport and get a few good shots." "Jesus Christ, Al," a TV man said. "If you go out there now you're going to be killed."

"Well," said Al Rockoff casually, picking up his cameras, "it wouldn't be for the first time."

The Chinese-made rockets the Khmer Rouge were pouring at a great rate into the airport, and less frequently into the centre of the sprawling city, in those days were psychological as well as physical weapons. They were meant mainly to create fear and they did.

They shot across the sky with a screaming sound and landed with an explosion that could be heard for miles. Their shells contained coils of twisted steel, as sharp as razor blades, which broke into small pieces of corkscrew-shaped shrapnel on impact and literally twisted the guts out of any unfortunate they hit. It was said that once you heard the scream in the sky the rocket was gone so you were safe and the queasy feeling in the stomach and urge to run somewhere, anywhere, were purposeless. But they still frightened the hell out of everyone, except perhaps Al Rockoff.

They usually came in pairs, so that when the photographers—and more occasionally we journalists—jumped in ancient rented cars and drove toward the sound of the first explosion to report on the deaths and damage, we had the fear that we were driving directly into the path of the second rocket.

For some reason we always felt fairly safe at the Hotel Le Phnom, although rockets were regularly hitting the Ministry of Information building only a few hundred yards away. The Hotel Monorom a little farther south was in a different situation. The Communists appeared to have a bead on it. Two correspondents who could not get rooms at the Le Phnom, Jack Reynolds of NBC and Frank Mariano of ABC, were forced to live on the top floors of the smaller hotel. They were the most nervous of us all.

One afternoon, one of the rockets hit right in the middle of a group of pedicab drivers waiting outside the hotel and ripped eight or ten of them to pieces. Their bodies were in such a mess it was impossible to know how many of them there had been. I was walking nearby when the rocket hit and I jumped in a pedicab and ordered its skinny puller to run toward the noise. He balked like a frightened horse after a few hundred yards but by then we were in

49

sight of the hotel and the carnage outside. Smoke was still pouring from the bodies on the roadway and there was half a body in the small, round, sandbagged bunker where the hotel guard did his duty. Later, Frank Mariano told me he was in the hotel lobby when the rocket hit, saw the guard in the bunker was wounded and ran to help him. But when he tried to lift the guard clear of the sandbags he found himself hugging only the top half of his body. The incident upset him and ABC sent their toughest old hand, Jim Bennett, to replace him. Frank died in California the following year. He was thirty-eight.

Soon after the rocket hit at the Monorom I decided it was close to time to leave. Broadcasts from the Khmer Rouge stating that foreign journalists would be considered "enemies of the people" and shot when Phnom Penh was captured helped me make up my mind.

But I had a conscience about two delightfully crazy Canadian girls, Dolly and Anna Charet, who simply refused to abandon the forty-two tiny children they were caring for at the orphanage they called Canada House. They were both scared stiff, because their spotlessly clean and efficient orphanage was not far from the central market, the object of many rocket attacks. Still they could not be persuaded by me, the Canadian Embassy in Thailand or the British Embassy in Cambodia to leave their babies in the care of Cambodian nuns and nurses and go home.

They would just stand there in the orphanage, scared, set smiles on their attractive faces, usually holding a baby and bottle, and shake their heads at the suggestion. "I'm going to stand in front of the Khmer Rouge troops if they come and tell them if they kill me they'll be killing our kids as well," Dolly said once. If she had guessed what the Khmer Rouge were to do when they got to Phnom Penh she might have felt differently.

But she meant it. The two well-to-do sisters from Montebello, Quebec, wouldn't listen to anybody. They were, I suppose, brave but they were also impossible. I cabled *The Toronto Star* at one stage suggesting we try to arrange a helicopter lift as a humanitarian stunt to take the girls and their babies (and incidentally me) to Saigon. But there was no reply from the foreign desk.

Weeks later, in the foyer of the Caravelle Hotel in Saigon, a young woman ran to throw her arms around me. She was weeping with excitement and it was a while before I realized it was Dolly. "We made it, Jack," she wept. "We made it. And we've got the kids with us."

She refused to say how she got the children out of Cambodia, putting her fingers to her lips conspiratorially and saying, "Shush." And next day when I saw the two sisters lining their little children up at Saigon's Tan Son Nhut airport for a flight that would eventually take them to Canada, they still refused to say how they arranged the miracle.

It was not easy for me to get out of Cambodia anyway, with or without the two girls. A USAID DC-3 was taking some Americans, including journalists, out on a daily flight to Saigon, but when I suggested to the US Embassy I'd like a ride I was told that no consideration was being given at the time to the evacuation of "third-country nationals."

There were still said to be daily flights to Saigon and Bangkok by Air Camboge's single Caravelle jet and an old DC-4. The airline's downtown terminal was jampacked with Cambodians carrying all they could crush into a few suitcases or string bags. They were willing to risk the rocket-run bus ride from the bunkered terminal to a bunker at Pontechong, and then a run across the open tarmac to the aircraft.

I waited on two mornings at the terminal with several other correspondents and the crowd of frightened Cambodians. But the planes never came. The Cambodians drifted away, stoical men with their arms around weeping wives and little wide-eyed children who seemed unaware of what was going on. Twice a grinning clerk re-welcomed me to the now almost empty Hotel Le Phnom. And twice the few remaining correspondents booed my return with a mixture of good humour and professional anguish, because I was supposed to be "pigeoning" their stories and film to wherever I could have them transmitted.

Except for once in a while, there was no electricity at the Le Phnom in those days. The old air conditioners rattled no more and the big ceiling fans were still. The big rooms with their bare tile floors were like incinerators and writing by candlelight was a sweaty, difficult business. But there was still reasonably good food at the little restaurant near the hotel's swimming pool and some particularly good French wine. There was also the inevitable Asian gaggle of good-looking girls, lounging in deck chairs on the lawn near the pool and smiling enticingly.

As a happily-married man I always avoided the women. It was probably easier for me than for some others. To begin with I had had a mild coronary in Hong Kong shortly before this assignment and my doctor had instructed me to avoid any undue stress and excitement. I was not too sure whether a shot of sexual excitement combined with the nervous stress of the overall situation would do me any good. And secondly, I am allergic to penicillin, a disastrous impediment to any active involvement with readily available Asian women.

Perhaps on this night though it was the French wine or just the feeling that life was short and lonely. She was half Chinese and half Cambodian. Although she must have been in her mid thirties, she was very beautiful and she acted in that dingy, candlelit hotel room as if it was one of her last nights on earth, which it probably was.

We were exactly and literally at the climax of our short but hectic relationship when a rocket hit about a hundred yards from the hotel, shaking the walls and scattering big, broken bits of ceiling plaster on us, the bed and the floor. In an instant, while the noise still reverberated and the building still shook, she threw me onto the floor, overturned the bed and pulled me under it, shaking while she hugged me on the cold tiles.

I've been confident ever since I will never have another heart attack. It would have happened then.

I got out of Phnom Penh, well before the city fell, on an Australian Air Force c-130, sent to evacuate Australian Embassy personnel, and I was glad to go. Denis Warner, the great Australian expert on Southeast Asia, a journalistic hero of my youth whom I'd never met before, escaped with me. He complained, as an embassy car drove us on a devious route through open fields to the airport, that the older he got the more right-wing were his views, creating a bias that was a journalistic nuisance.

The timing was terrific. The Australians had, of course, brought some beer along but there was time only for one Foster's lager before the big plane touched down on a back section of the airport. The pilots kept the motors running. There were some burned-out skeletons of planes nearby and a wrecked World Airlines dc-8, one of the shuttle that had been bringing American-sponsored rice to the besieged city. Two rockets hit the airport as we boarded the plane. We were lumbering off and zig-zagging away within minutes.

Some correspondents stayed. Syd Schanberg of *The New York Times* stayed. He wanted to win a Pulitzer Prize and he did. Claude Juvenal and Jean Jacques Cazeau, of Agence France Presse stayed. They wrote the final stories, the best ones. Young Jon Swain, a freelancer for the London *Sunday Times,* came to my hotel room in Saigon a week or so after I left Cambodia, told me he was thinking of going into Phnom Penh and asked for my advice. I told him not to go, it would be madness.

"I've got to make a name for myself," he said. "It's the only way the *Sunday Times* will put me on staff."

Peter Kent then of the Canadian Broadcasting Corporation went in, leaving his bags in my hotel room in Saigon for safekeeping. He came out with the American helicopter evacuation as Phnom Penh was falling. So did Tony Paul, of *Reader's Digest.* They were all mad and they all got great stories, but those who bravely stayed to face the Khmer Rouge missed the big one, the fall of Saigon two weeks later.

Swain was only twenty-seven years old and was more of an adventurer than a journalist. When he was fifteen he had run away from his middle-class British home to join the Foreign Legion, in which his older brother was a sergeant and therefore one of the world's toughest men. A relative followed him to Corsica, however, hauled him by the scruff of the neck from the Legion's parade ground and took him home. He had been in Indochina for five years learning his journalism backwards as a freelancer, picking up the tricks of the trade in the field before he'd really learned to write. But he was keen, brave, good-looking and hard-working and his peers liked him and helped him. He would sometimes come to my room with a story before he filed it asking for advice about style and muttering: "I wish I could write like you chaps do."

But he had learned early the main trick of the trade—
to be in the right place at the right time—and from Phnom
Penh he laid down the facts of one of history's most pathetic and puzzling disasters in a simple diary form that
made one of the best stories of the decade.

In his story that was splashed over four pages in the
London *Sunday Times,* Swain wrote:

Thursday, April 17, 1975—6:00 a.m:

The city of Phnom Penh awoke to a richly-coloured dawn.
But from the Monivong bridge in the south to the spruce
white villas around the Hotel Le Phnom, buildings trem-
bled to the shock of rockets and shells.

A few minutes after 6:00 a.m., the chief telex operator
at the post office—where I was sending my last dispatch to
The Sunday Times—learned that his little girl had been
killed by artillery fire near the Chamcar Mon palace and his
wife had been fatally injured. He had worked all night to
send our last dispatches on an extraordinary emergency
transmitter made in China before the fall of Shanghai.
Dressing hurriedly, uttering not a word, he went outside.
As he passed, a limp figure in the sunlight, we averted our
eyes.

7:00 a.m:

The crackle of small-arms fire was coming closer to the
Hotel Le Phnom—declared a Red Cross international security zone, and packed with an uneasy mixture of Cambodians and foreigners. From its second-floor windows refugees could be seen streaming into the city. Among them
were soldiers who had thrown away their guns. A squadron
of armoured personnel carriers (APCs) regrouped around

the hotel. They had come from the collapsed northern front. It was unclear whether they should fight or surrender.

The insurgent radio, broadcasting a message to the people ("We are ready to welcome you") was the first sign that the Khmer Rouge were entering the city. Then Pascal, a Red Cross doctor, burst into the lobby saying there were some Khmer Rouge near the French Embassy half a mile away. As he ran upstairs for his passport, mortar bombs fell a few streets away. The din of battle mounted and the refugees in the hotel grounds huddled closer together. The government radio began playing French military music—meant, presumably, to summon one last drop of patriotic fervour. The Khmer Rouge were at the extreme end of the Monivong Boulevard. They fired a B40 rocket at the car of a two-star general desperately seeking asylum in the French Embassy. The rocket tore a hole in the embassy gate and the general beat a hasty retreat.

By 7:50 the government radio was going on and off the air. The people in the street on the north side of the hotel suddenly began to run. And at about this time M. Adolphe Lesnik, the director of an Anglo-French tobacco company in Phnom Penh, looked out of his apartment window some five hundred yards from the hotel and saw "a little chap all in black" walk purposefully down the street. M. Lesnik was witnessing the arrival of the first Khmer Rouge soldier. "The fellow stopped outside the ammunition depot opposite my building and yelled to the soldiers who were preparing to defend it, 'You can shoot me easily, but if you do you'll all die. There are many more men behind me. Come out now, be sensible and surrender.' "

M. Lesnik saw the Cambodian soldiers stack their weapons and come out—not despondently, but with joy and applause. Khmer Rouge called at M. Lesnik's building and asked the guardian if any Americans were there. Only French, the guardian replied truthfully. The soldier went smiling away, telling him to put up white flags. White flags were beginning to sprout everywhere—on APCs drawn up outside the hotel, on houses in the northern section of the city that the Khmer Rouge had just penetrated. And yellow alamanda blossoms covered the headlamps of the half-tracks. Clearly the Cambodian army was about to pack up after five years of war. Troops took out the clips of their M16 rifles and waited quietly in the sunlight for the insurgents.

8:50 a.m:

With fighting noises still coming from the southern part of the city, a crowd gathered in the Monivong Boulevard outside the French Embassy. It stretched right across the road, and in the centre of it was a young man in black with a flat, round face and a white scarf. The soldiers and townspeople around him joined hands, hoisted him onto their shoulders and bore him triumphantly to an APC. Western photographers and a mixed group of soldiers and civilians climbed up with this Khmer Rouge soldier. The APC moved down the boulevard, past the hotel, seeming to carry a message of peace.

For a moment there was hope. Then at 9:04 precisely, a mortar crash tore the air. The splash of smoke outside the Hotel Monorom, a few hundred yards in front of the APCs, had hardly cleared when another mortar-bomb burst— closer this time. A machine gun knocked harshly. The APC slewed around and roared back the way it had come. Photographers, soldiers and people scurried like crabs for cover. The Khmer Rouge, it seemed, were welcome in one part of the city, and met with force in another.

For the next twenty minutes fighting swirled through

the streets around the Hotel Le Phnom. A Red Cross stretcher team rushed a wounded soldier through a lobby full of people cowering from stray bullets. Hardly more than a boy, he had a small, black hole in the side of his head. In the bungalow that the Scottish medical team had converted into an operating theatre, surgeon Michael Daly, of Glasgow, took one look and shook his head. "He has a bullet in the brain. There is nothing we can do." At 9:20 the soldier coughed up a stream of blood. His hands fluttered, and with a shudder he died. Daly and his team moved on without a pause to the next casualty, a civilian with a bullet in the lung.

10:00 a.m:

There was a commotion outside. Prince Sirik Matak, one of the seven "arch traitors" of the old regime, condemned to death by the Khmer Rouge, was among scores of refugees trying to fight their way into the hotel. Red Cross officials manning the gates politely refused him entry, on the grounds that his presence would endanger the lives of others. The prince, dressed in a short-sleeved, beige T-shirt and slacks, spoke briefly to reporters about the fighting. "You see there are personalities who are determined to resist. We do not want a Communist government here." He left in evident distress and we learned later that the French Embassy had granted him asylum.

Soon the fighting died in the north of the city and people began to come out into the streets. They wore *chromas,* the checked scarves which are the symbol of friendship in rural Cambodia. Soldiers on both sides rode through the streets on the tops of half-tracks. "Hey, Mister Journalist take our picture," they cried. Everyone seemed to be filled—deceptively—with a sense of joy at the end of the war. We saw a smiling, saffron-robed monk ride in a jeep with a Khmer Rouge, and through an interpreter we learned that the new Communist regime would respect Buddhism. The fighting in the north of the city now seemed to be over and Khmer Rouge soldiers, hardly more than boys, were riding around in a host of vehicles including ambulances.

With a certain amount of misgiving I walked the quarter of a mile to the post office only to find it deserted, its communications down. However, outside in the sunny Provence-like square a Khmer Rouge soldier pedalled by on a bicycle. He wore the usual soft Mao hat, green fatigues and a cheap pair of field glasses. The pistol on his belt indicated he was an officer. He smiled politely at us but refused to accept our gifts of oranges and cigarettes. "The corrupt and the traitors will have to be punished," he said. "But I can assure you there will be no bloodbath."

Meanwhile, at the Olympic Stadium, a number of senior army officers and politicians, including the supreme commander, General Sak Sutsakhan, were making their getaway. The helicopters had been standing by for thirty-six hours, fuelled, ready to go. They clattered into the air as the first Khmer Rouge soldiers were pushing into the stadium, bazookas and rifles at the ready.

Intense fighting was still going on in the western quarters of the town near the airport, where the crack Cambodian Paratroop Brigade prepared for a final stand. A key figure in this was the French mercenary, Dominique Borella, an ex-foreign legionary and a veteran of France's own wars in Algeria and Indochina. He had made the Cambodian cause his own and over the last six months had been thrice wounded. He lived and fought with the paras for very little pay. Now this blond giant helped direct the last defence of the brigade headquarters on the edge of the airport. When it finally crumbled late in the morning he shed his uniform and sneaked into the city. His girlfriend fixed him up with some civilian clothes and, resourceful to the last, he sought refuge in the French Embassy. Back at the para headquarters, the brigade commander shot himself.

11:00 a.m:

It now seemed safe to wander around the central part of the town. The Khmer Rouge, who were firmly in control, seemed to be a friendly enough lot, and with some colleagues I headed for the Ministry of Information where we had learned there was a gathering of Khmer Rouge military leaders. A curious sight greeted us. Holding court on the grass, outside the long, colonial-style building was a young man in black, with a handsome, angular face. In impeccable French he introduced himself as Hem Keth Dara, son of a former minister. Dara described himself as the commanding general of the nationalist movement that had "liberated" the city. He had been educated in Paris and was married to a Frenchwoman who was in France. He was twenty-nine and had been in Phnom Penh since 1971. This arrogant playboy could hardly be a revolutionary and it was inconceivable that he fitted the tough mould of the Khmer Rouge movement. He gave orders all the time, telling the young, black-clad soldiers around the building to move back and stay still. When they pushed forward again he brandished a pistol in a Hollywood fashion that commanded only token respect.

"I took Phnom Penh with only three hundred men. We suffered no casualties," he boasted. Then, dismissing us with a wave of his pistol, he told us to listen to broadcast announcements. "The city must be reorganized before you can send dispatches," he said. Both he and his soldiers struck a false note. They were too neat and too friendly by far to be genuine Khmer Rouge straight from the hills.

Now worrying, conflicting reports began to come in about the true identity of the Khmer Rouge units. It seemed that there were already at least two factions. Those in the north (including the amazing Mr. Dara) were chummy. Reports from the southern end of the city, where sporadic fighting still continued, told of a very tough force of insurgents that had moved in and was busy digging foxholes. It was pushing refugees out of the city and seemed to be deploying itself for battle. The implication was that the troops in the north were nationalists, those in the south hardline Communists, but this was obviously too simplistic. Mr. Dara and his merry band were presumably opportunists who had misjudged the true mettle of the Khmer Rouge. An American photographer who visited the southern sector said the Khmer Rouge there were grim and seasoned soldiers. Their mud-stained feet and uniforms showed they had not been pussy-footing around. He said they were disarming government soldiers, stacking all weapons in huge piles, throwing away the boots, and marching the men out of the city to unknown destinations.

12:30 p.m:

It was now the hottest time of the day. Hundreds of people were being subjected to a hideous death at the Preah Ket Melea Hospital. The doctors had not reported to work for two days and there was no one to treat the two thousand wounded. People by the dozen were bleeding to death in the corridors, the floors of the wards were caked with blood. The hot, fetid air was thick with flies—the sight of these swarming over the living and the dead, over the anguished faces of those who knew they were doomed to die, churned the stomach. I asked a distraught nurse for an explanation. Wringing her hands as the plasma bottles and saline drips emptied one by one, she said: "I phoned the doctors. They say they are coming in a short time, but they are not here yet. Maybe they are afraid.''

The work of the Scottish team, who had filled a ward with sophisticated equipment and brightened it with children's pictures on the walls, was wiped out in these scenes of horror. Upstairs it was worse. The dead and the dying lay in pools of their own blood. The long corridor outside the operating theatre was literally awash with it. Here a man and his wife died in each others arms. A few feet away an old man was pushed up against the wall, his intestines tumbling out like laundry. Further down the corridor was a soldier with an arm, head and stomach wound, a Khmer Rouge who had somehow been brought there for treatment. A single harassed doctor fussed impotently around. It was easy to see that but for our presence he would have already gone home. The Khmer Rouge croaked through fly-blown lips: "Water, water, please get me some water." We couldn't because of his stomach wound. Hospital workers with scrubbing brushes and bowls of soapy water started to wash the blood off the floor. They brushed between the legs of the corpses and sent the red mixture splashing down the open lift shaft.

With one accord my companions and I, Sydney Schanberg of the *New York Times,* freelance American photographer Al Rockoff, and a Cambodian interpreter, sloshed our way through the blood to the exit.

1:00 p.m:

We emerged into the heat to find people running away from the front gate. We drove slowly towards the street, but before we could reach it there came a rushing of steps and half a dozen Khmer Rouge soldiers, bristling with guns, dragged us out of the car and pushed us and shook their rifles at us. They were boys, hardly taller than their tightly-held AK47 rifles, but their ignorance made them super-deadly. Their leader was a cold ill-tempered man with a pistol. He held it to my head, screaming and ranting. His finger was tight on the trigger. His eyes were coals of hate. Life seemed to be over and I stood there paralysed with fear. We had, I thought, got up this morning like everybody else, but because we had been foolish enough to leave the hotel we would never see the end of the day. Our hands were high in the air. Our cameras, notebooks and other belongings littered the drive where the Khmer Rouge had thrown them. A chastened, very frightened band we moved to what we imagined to be our execution. They took us away in an armoured personnel carrier with the top hatch and rear door both bolted shut, and we sat there in the gummy heat and waited for them to toss in a grenade and finish us off.

That they did not kill us is due to the courage and devotion of Sydney Schanberg's Cambodian interpreter, Dith Pran. Mr. Pran explained that the Khmer Rouge had told him he was free to go—that they were only after the rich and the bourgeoisie. But knowing they intended to kill us, he insisted on staying. So, too, did our chauffeur.

We rode through the streets, then stopped and picked up two more prisoners, Cambodians in civilian clothes. The big one with the moustache and crew-cut wore a white T-shirt and jeans. The smaller man was clad in a sports shirt and slacks. Both were officers and quite as frightened as we were. The big man we recognized as second-in-command of the navy. He desperately tried to give us his wallet. We told him it was no use, and finally he hid it in the back of the APC. The smaller man put an ivory Buddha in his mouth as a talisman. We were all sweating furiously, both from the heat and fear. Sydney Schanberg took out of his pocket a crumpled bit of cloth, an artificial rose that was a gift from his daughter a couple of weeks before. "As long as I've got this, we'll be all right," he said, forcing a thin smile. I did not share his faith.

The top hatch unfolded with a bang and a man, pointing a gun at me, screamed "We are not Vietnamese. We don't like Vietnamese." It was an odd thing to say as so far I had been speaking only French to establish that I was not American. But perhaps the Khmer Rouge thought I was talking Vietnamese. Evidently he harboured the traditional Cambodian hatred for his neighbours.

1:40 p.m:

The APC shuddered to a halt. Bolts slid back, the rear door was opened and we saw water and a pair of Khmer Rouge soldiers, holding rifles on us, beckoning for us to come. We stared at each other. We were sure we were going to be executed and our bodies tossed into the river. Eyes blinking, we stepped out into the sunlight. Nothing happened— but immediately Dith Pran, the interpreter, began to talk and talk. It was marvellous to see him explain our case. He spoke softly and firmly, and by and by the tension went out of the air. We were ordered to stand across the street from the river and wait. We drank water from a bucket and watched people stream out of the city up Route Five. We assumed they were refugees returning to their homes. In fact the Khmer Rouge had issued orders for the entire city to be evacuated.

The troops had also started to loot, a process that was to continue for days. Soldiers drove past in cars heaped high with cigarettes, soft drinks and wines. Few knew how to drive: the crash of gear boxes was the prevailing sound. In other circumstances their efforts to make the cars go would have been hilarious. Now they were grotesque: the peasant boys with death at the tip of their fingers were behaving like spoiled brats. They seemed to be every bit as irresponsible as the Cambodian army they had defeated.

At 3:30 p.m. a man of some authority ordered us released, and most of our belongings were returned. The insurgents kept the car, my notebooks, films and hotel key. We were much too tired to argue. Hitching a ride with two Frenchmen, we drove straight to the Ministry of Information—where, we understood, there was to be a news conference.

4:00 p.m:

Here was a very different scene from the morning. Colourful Mr. Dara was there, but he was no longer in charge. He was unarmed and a semi-prisoner. The cocky expression had vanished from his face. He looked tired and uneasy. There were fifty prisoners lined up in front of the building. They included Lon Non, Marshall Lon Nol's younger brother and one of the most corrupt, hated members of the old regime. There were several generals, and Hou Hang Sin, director of the cabinet of Long Boret. But the prime minister was absent although no one doubted he was still in the city. He had sworn he would stay to the end, although it meant certain death.

Meanwhile, the tempo of looting of shops, business premises and private homes mounted. The governor of the Banque Khmer de Commerce was sitting quietly in his office ready to hand over the keys of the safe to Phnom Penh's new rulers. A group of soldiers burst in, booted him into the street and, according to eye witnesses, ransacked the entire place. They burned the records and millions upon millions of riels. There was to be no place for money in the Cambodian peasant revolution.

Back at the information ministry a man in black, about thirty, and clearly a leader, bawled through a bullhorn at the prisoners, dividing them into three groups: military, political, and ordinary civilians. Khmer Rouge training their guns on them were tough, strong-looking, in jungle-green Mao hats and the inevitable Ho Chi Minh sandals. Each one was a walking arsenal. To us, standing there, they looked like people from another planet. Now the leader talked to the prisoners. He told them there were only seven "arch-traitors" and that they were not to consider themselves captives but as surrendered people. He pledged there would be no reprisals. As he talked a squad of soldiers, not more than thirteen years old, crouched in combat positions among the trees, menacing us and the prisoners with their guns. Three old ladies from the Cambodian Red Cross, dressed up and perfumed as if for a party, came forward and offered their co-operation. They too might have come from another world.

The tension eased. Briefly the Khmer Rouge leader, who smilingly declined to volunteer his name, broke off to speak to the press. "I represent the armed forces," he said. Then spontaneously he praised the American people. "We wish to thank the American people and all the people in the world who love peace and justice. The American people have helped us and supported us since March 18, 1970." (The date when Prince Sihanouk's government fell to a coup encouraged by the US government.)

"Will you kill Americans as the US Embassy has predicted?" a journalist asked.

"We respect prisoners of war. That is our military position."

He said he had no idea what the political leaders would do. He was a soldier in the Cambodian National Liberation Army and his duty was to secure the city. Later the politicians would come. As he spoke guns rattled in some parts of the city.

4:50 p.m:

A black Citroen pulled up and [Prime Minister] Mr. Long Boret, his eyes puffy and red, got out. His face was empty of expression. When we asked him how he was he muttered a short incoherent sentence. His thoughts were elsewhere. Dazed, legs wobbling, he surrendered to the Khmer Rouge. One could not fail to admire his courage.

4:55 p.m:

Without warning Khmer Rouge soldiers forced their way into our quarters in the Hotel Le Phnom, menacing the inmates with B40 rockets. Summoning André Pasquier, the chief Red Cross delegate, they told him harshly to empty the place within half-an-hour. Wild soldiers rushed into the Scottish medical team's operating theatre, demanding cartons of medicines. They rummaged through cupboards and drank several bottles of intravenous serum. In the next room nurse Pat Ash stripped a wounded government soldier of his uniform and put it roughly over a dead man. Otherwise it was obvious the soldier would have been shot.

Pandemonium gripped the hotel. People ran in all directions. What did it mean? Where would they go? The general consensus was to the French Embassy down the road.

The poor refugees in the garden gathered their cooking pots and hit the road; clearly they were destined for the countryside and an uncertain future. So too were the hotel staff, who clutched imploringly at foreigners' arms. "Don't abandon us," they cried. But there was no time to talk. Already the Khmer Rouge soldiers, squat and sinister, were at the gate with guns. I joined the trail of refugees, forgetting all thoughts of getting into my room and collecting my belongings. Many troops were in the city now. As we headed

up the Monivong Boulevard towards the [French] embassy
a fresh battalion marched Indian-file into the town. They
were well-armed, disciplined troops, marching with the
swagger of victors, staring straight ahead.

6:30 p.m:

Dusk closed in. People were jumping over the high embassy wall, handing their children over, tossing over their
belongings. It was a mob scene. An Indian fell off the wall
and broke his leg. Outside in the darkening street the people streamed out of the city in their thousands. The road
past the embassy was thick with them. Abandoned cars, discarded shoes littered their path.

The French consul, Jean Dyrac, driving out to pick up
some French friends, had the tricolour ripped from his car
by angry Khmer Rouge soldiers. The unthinkable was happening. In their zest for revolution the Khmer Rouge sol-
dier-peasantry had not embarked on a bloodbath as the
Americans always claimed they would. Instead they were
emptying the city of its two million people. There have
been few precedents for such behaviour and the reason
they did it is still obscure.

V

The Reporters' Escape

WHEN YOU THINK YOU ARE going to die a helpless numbness sets in along with the fear. There is just not much you can do about it and you hope that it comes quickly and painlessly. But somewhere deep in this numbness you wonder what you have done wrong to get yourself in the position you're in, what you should have done differently and why the hell you are where you are instead of covering city hall at home. If the experience is drawn out over time, as it was for Swain and Schanberg, as the Khmer Rouge first held guns to their heads and then took them away in the APC, apparently to be executed, a little hope returns after a while and even professionalism. "If I get out of this," you say to yourself, "it will be a part of the story."

But you wonder mainly whether you've been stupid. It's not the journalist's job to get killed or even to get into trouble. His job is the opposite, to calmly observe occurrences around him, from as safe a place as possible and close to his communications. He has to step aside from it all, uninvolved, seeking the perspective. Dead reporters don't file stories. So there's no heroism there, just this helplessness combined with the thought that you must not do anything to hasten your death. Then when it's finished a shaking fear follows the calmer fear of the bad moments, and then a small amount of euphoria takes over. For a little while you feel immortal. And then you go about your business as best you can in the circumstances.

Young Jon Swain continued his Phnom Penh diary:

Friday, April 18—7:00 a.m:

The Khmer Rouge army is emptying the city and its hospitals—tipping out patients like garbage into the streets. Bandaged men and women hobble by the embassy. Wives push wounded soldier husbands on hospital beds on wheels, some with serum drips still attached. In five years of war this is the greatest caravan of human misery I have seen. The Khmer Rouge must know that few of the 20,000 wounded will survive. One can only conclude that they have no humanitarian instincts. The entire city is being emptied of its people: the old, the sick, the infirm, the hungry, the orphans, without exception.

Only the French Embassy will remain. Already about 1,500 people are sheltering in it and more refugees are still jumping over the wall. They told me the Khmer Rouge came into their shops and offices at gunpoint and forced them to leave. One Frenchman, who made it this morning, says:

Right through the night Khmer Rouge soldiers were trying to force their way into my shop. They fired at the main door with an automatic rifle. They reversed a truck into the gate but it was too stout. This morning an officer told me firmly I must leave at once. I have lost everything.

The French consul, M. Jean Dyrac, has been up all night on the radio to Paris. We foreigners are in the reception hall and relatively well off. The air conditioning and water supplies are still working. But the embassy compound outside is choked with hundreds of Cambodians, Vietnamese and Chinese, camping like Gypsies on the grass. They are hungry and afraid. Many French families are living in cars. Whichever way you turn there are people. The spacious gardens of tamarinds and palms are black with them. The embassy gates are locked. I have never seen so much anguish on a man's face as on the consul's today as he turns people away.

Murray Carmichael, the anaesthetist in the Scottish medical team, says:

Three-quarters of our work has been wasted. We spent so much time treating patients who had been badly operated on, lying in bed getting thin and wasted. We taught them to walk again, put them on traction and got some union into their bones. The Khmer Rouge told them to leave in ten minutes. These people have no compassion, no humanity. They are just here to do it their own way and it's nasty. We performed only one operation under the new regime, saving a man who had been shot through the throat. Then we had to abandon him.

10:45 a.m:

Water in the compound runs out. Khmer Rouge soldiers are outside the gates of the embassy demanding to come in. One man enters, dressed in black. He shakes hands with Dyrac and goes inside the chancellery.

There is a lot of sporadic firing in the city. The Khmer Rouge seem to be using up more ammunition than they ever did in the war. Soldiers are driving up and down outside the embassy in half-tracks, peering through its wall. The Khmer Rouge Army has discipline. It is the discipline that says the new order is right, that anything in the way of that order must be eliminated and cast out. It is not the discipline that respects human life and people's property.

11:30 a.m:

A us Phantom makes two high-level runs over the city. We hope it will not provoke the Khmer Rouge. Presumably it is taking pictures.

A newly-arrived French teacher says that at 8:30 this morning he was on his way to the embassy when a Khmer Rouge patrol ran out of an alley and cut a line of refugees in half, splitting a family. When the parents protested he raised his rifle and shot them in their chests. The teacher also said the Khmer Rouge fired on anyone who looked out of his balcony during the night.

1:30 p.m:

André Pasquier, chief Red Cross delegate in Phnom Penh, has the jitters. He thinks the Red Cross is in bad odour with the Khmer Rouge because it sheltered refugees in the Hotel Le Phnom right up to the end. The Khmer Rouge seem to feel that by providing medical aid to the Phnom Penh regime the Red Cross prolonged the war. I hear Pasquier saying to another Red Cross man, Gustav Streiffert, "Do you think we will be court martialled?"

The conventional wisdom used to be that the Hanoi old guard who went to North Vietnam in 1954 controlled the Khmer Rouge, and that the Khmer Rouge Rumdos, the pro-Sihanouk nationalist faction, was being run down. Now

Author Jack Cahill and photographer Boris Spremo with South Vietnamese soldiers in what was left of Quang Tri, a city of over 60,000 people, after American B52 bombings (1973).

Minutes after a rocket attack in Phnom Penh, Cambodia, the newsmen are on the spot, risking a second attack that usually followed. On the left is Neil Davis, on the right Jon Swain of The London Sunday Times.

Photo by Sunday Times of London

Jon Swain in Vietnam, 1975.

Women smuggling gasoline across the Thai border to the Khmer Rouge in Cambodia in 1976. They came back with Scotch whisky and French wine.

Khmer Rouge soldiers inspect wares smuggled across the bridge at Poipet that separates Cambodia from Thailand, near Aranyapathet, in 1976. The Khmers pointed rifles at the author as he took the picture with a 200 mm. long-distance lens.

Refugee children on the "Trail of Tears." They were part of a group that gathered in a rubber plantation outside the South Vietnamese village of Trang Bom in April, 1975, after a circuitous walk through jungle that took two to three days.

Refugees poured towards Saigon after Xuan Loc, about thirty-five miles north of Saigon, fell to the Communists on April 21, 1975. South Vietnamese authorities turned them away from Saigon when they arrived there.

The night before Danang fell to the North Vietnamese its population had more than doubled by the flow of refugees from the fighting further north.

These refugees managed to escape from Danang and travel by barge to Vung Tau, south of Saigon. The bundle the young man is carrying is his mother, who died on the journey.

Refugees from Danang arriving at Vung Tau, south of Saigon, in April 1975.

A Communist tank crashes through the gates of the presidential palace in Saigon, marking the end of the Vietnam War. The Associated Press picture may have been taken by TV cameraman and correspondent Neil Davis, the only journalist present as the Viet Cong took over the palace.

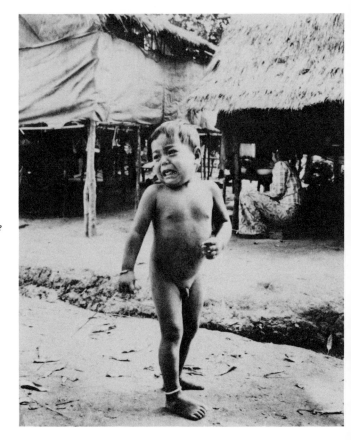

Millions of Cambodians fled the Khmer Rouge genocide in 1976, including this child (right) in a refugee camp in Thailand.

Author Jack Cahill, four days out from Saigon on the refugee ship, Sgt. Miller, *in the South China Sea.*

Some of the "roundeye family" on the Sgt. Miller *take their turn sheltering from the sun under a small canopy made of sheets. Left to right, Mike Sullivan of the BBC, Vietnamese bargirl Anne-Marie Disloquez, and English-French socialite Renée Schiller.*

At least 7,000 refugees crowded the small cargo ship, attempting to shelter from the searing sun. Water was rationed to about two small cups a day and sometimes the daily ration of rice mixed with a little fish or meat didn't arrive. Nobody died. Four children were born.

The crowded holds of the Sgt. Miller "smelled like a wet diaper."

I don't know what to think. Sihanouk's name is hardly mentioned, but nor is communism. All Khmer Rouge I have spoken to say they are nationalists.

Adolphe Lesnik tells a typical hardship tale. When the Khmer Rouge ordered out everyone in his building:

I telephoned the consul and he said put out French flags and posters saying you are French. Later we locked the doors and organized a night vigil. During the evening Khmer Rouge soldiers, drunk as only one can imagine a person to be drunk and still able to walk, got into the car park. They wanted to drive away our cars but they didn't have the keys. So they spent the whole night tooting horns, putting lights on. We stayed absolutely silent.

I did my watch until about 5:00 a.m. and was about to stretch out when in rushed my servant saying, "Be careful, there are women soldiers and they are very dangerous. They are shooting all over the place." As she spoke five women in black came in.

They fired into the air and they shouted "Everyone out immediately." I couldn't get the French Embassy on the phone. The women pointed their weapons at me and pointed at my watch indicating I had ten minutes to pack. I already had my briefcase packed and I chucked a few shirts into an airbag, but the women would not let me open a cupboard. When ten minutes was up they said "Out." I wanted to take some wine and whisky. But they fired a burst through the window and pointed their guns at my stomach.

Then I understood I had to get out. As I was going one of the women stopped me and looked at my watch. I pretended I could not unbuckle it. She unbuckled it for me and took it, then she indicated she wanted the keys to all cars. It was all done by sign language, fingers and guns.

73

Like many French *colons* Lesnik's history is fantastic. He says he saw the Japanese war in Manchuria in the 1930s, was imprisoned in China during the Second World War, and was in Shanghai in 1947 when it fell to the Communists. "But this is enough," he says. "I'm going home to Montpelier."

6:00 p.m:

Paul Ignatieff, the Canadian who is head of the UNICEF mission in Phnom Penh, calls a meeting of all us "Internationals." This includes the twenty-two journalists in the compound, fifteen members of the Red Cross including the Scottish medical team, six United Nations officials and a handful of other nationalities including Americans. He tells us the consul has made "pretty significant progress" during two meetings with the Khmer Rouge authorities, who call themselves the *Comité De La Ville*.

"The Khmer Rouge he is dealing with are very intelligent, dedicated and serious people. We are a small problem to them and it is encouraging that they have taken some time out to come and see us." Paul's briefing is immensely cheering. But Monsieur Morin, the vice-consul, has complained about people using up water for bathing. I ask him if he objects to us organizing security and water conservation for the "Internationals." "Go ahead," he says, "you're serious guys."

We are shut off from the outside world. Our sole links are the embassy radio and the BBC, which we listen to breathlessly. The BBC cites Chau Seng, Sihanouk's spokesman in Paris, as saying members of the Lon Nol regime in Phnom Penh will be judged in a humanitarian way. There will be no bloodshed. And the BBC wrongly reports from Bangkok that Long Boret was arrested as he boarded a helicopter.

There is always someone who doesn't play the game in an adverse situation. Tonight I saw a Frenchman come into the kitchen, open the fridge, take out one of our last steaks and toss it to his dog.

One of the most dejected members of our community on this, our first day in captivity, is perhaps its most experienced, Fernand Scheller, chief of the UN development project in Phnom Penh. He nearly weeps as he tells us how he has seen his Cambodian family and workers banished with everyone else to the countryside. "I have spent the whole day betraying my friends," he said.

What the Khmer Rouge are doing is pure and simple genocide. They will kill more people this way than if there had been fighting in the city. There is no food outside. The next rice crop is not until December, and anyway without outside help they can grow only enough to feed 30 per cent of the population. I have forty-two people standing by in Bangkok to come in. I am ready to help them—not them, the people. What is going on now is an example of demagoguery that makes one vomit.

Touring the embassy grounds I count about one hundred cars that families, mostly French, are using as makeshift homes. Smoke rises from scores of wood fires. The embassy is like one giant refuse dump. Dogs and children are everywhere. One person, however, is in equilibrium: the old French teacher we used to see daily at Le Phnom. She sits in a long white gown, fanning herself.

6:15 p.m:

The city is pretty quiet now, but the looting goes on. The Khmer Rouge soldiery is taking what it wants. One soldier I see pushing a "liberated" bicycle is wearing a long, crimson, winter overcoat. Yet the Khmer Rouge make an impressive contrast to the soldiers we used to see in Phnom Penh, drinking and whoring every night.

8:10 p.m:

Khmer Rouge soldiers outside the gates are making a din, tooting horns. It seems they cannot start the abandoned cars so they are bashing them in.

8:40 p.m:

We hear bangs and machine-gun fire from the direction of the airport. There is a fire in the west, not dense. Perhaps it is houses.

Saturday, April 19—7:00 a.m:

At the request of the Khmer Rouge the consul has begun to list all the people in the embassy. The Americans are worried. So too are the Cambodians who fear the Khmer Rouge will come in and get them.

10:00 a.m:

Drama within a drama. Mike Daly decides he must operate on a Cambodian soldier with an infected neck wound who is in the compound. The Khmer Rouge authorities have refused him permission to use Calmette, the French hospital next door, and the only one in the city still functioning. So he lies him out on a dining room sideboard, covered in a best linen tablecloth. He uses instruments off a silver tray. A lampstand becomes a drip support. The operation begins at 10:35 with children watching through a window. Halfway through Mike shakes his head at me. The man will die. When it happens, at 11:55, his wife next door lets out a terrible cry. She is inconsolable. A small party of us go out into the garden, dig a grave and bury him. Mike partly blames the death on the Khmer Rouge who refused to let him collect blood transfusion equipment. We are all very cast down.

We hear our first massacre story from a French doctor who says that when he went to his home, one mile north of Phnom Penh, he found it smashed down by a half-track and his nine children mown down inside. He thought the Khmer Rouge slaughtered his children when they were too frightened to open the door.

4:00 p.m:

According to the BBC the Khmer Rouge are still mopping up pockets of resistance in the provinces, and to nobody's surprise a spokesman for Sihanouk in Peking denies reports of Phnom Penh's evacuation. At least someone in the Khmer Rouge movement recognizes that what has happened is immoral and must be hidden.

5:35 p.m:

French consular staff, organizing accommodation, move us "Internationals" into the ambassador's residence. The *Salle de Reception*, our old abode, is given over to the French staff of Calmette Hospital who are tonight being thrown out. For the first time since the city's fall, we relax a little, drinking brandy and reading *Playboy* magazines to the sound of Martin Bloecher, of the Asian Christian Service, on the piano. Our new quarters are luxurious were it not that we are sleeping twenty to a room on cushions and chairs. Our room is lit with chandeliers. We drink from cut-glass goblets, and sharp-eyed Ignatieff has managed to "liberate" the cases of scotch and champagne from the cellar. But food is desperately scarce. A couple of bowls of rice is all I have eaten for two days.

This wretched place contains probably more than a

million dollars worth of cash and gold, smuggled in suit-cases and stashed away by refugees. The Khmer Rouge outside have no money, having burnt or confiscated all they can lay their hands on and reverted to the barter system. But one of them at least, I'm glad to say, is not adverse to a bit of bribery. An Indian businessman says he paid a Khmer Rouge one thousand dollars not to execute him.

6:22 p.m:

A column of fresh troops marches into the city. Refugees hurry the other way, crushed by fear. But their children giggle as they push trolleys of luggage down the road. For some at least this is a fun day.

6:25 p.m:

Big explosions rock the city. Plumes of smoke ring it like funeral pyres.

6:40 p.m:

The French staff of Calmette Hospital arrive with more accounts of cruelty and madness. For two days, they say, they operated ceaselessly on Communist wounded while looking down the barrels of guns. "The Khmer Rouge threatened to kill me if I didn't save the life of one man," said surgeon Bernard Piquart. Other witnesses corroborated this story. "A gun was placed to my head and a grenade dangled before my nose. Finally the Khmer Rouge threw us all out after smashing in the medicine cabinets with their rifle butts."

Sunday, April 20—8:00 a.m:

I awake this morning to find the Scottish Red Cross team playing bridge in the garden. This draws the usual absurd wisecracks about the nonchalance of Brits in a tight spot.

8:35 a.m:

The Khmer Rouge authorities notify the consul they no longer consider this to be an embassy. They say it is an international regroupment centre for all foreigners. Dyrac tells all Cambodian refugees here they must leave in the interests of self-preservation. He is concerned that if they stay the Khmer Rouge will come in and execute them on the spot. He says he has raised with Paris the question of our urgent evacuation and requested the *Comité De La Ville* to give us food. The loss of embassy status wrecks the last hope the Cambodians had of permanently sheltering here. They take the news badly.

Hundreds of Cambodians, Vietnamese, Chinese, pack up a few belongings and leave. We share our food with them. With heavy hearts we watch them trudge out of the embassy gate to an uncertain future. The Khmer Rouge have split up whole families—French husbands can stay, but Cambodian wives and children must go. The feeling of helplessness and rage is overwhelming. Is nothing sacred? We turn away as those about to be separated cling together, fighting back their tears. Suddenly it rains. It usually does at funerals.

I turn around and find the American Doug Sapper, one of the toughest, bravest men I know, a decorated ex-Green Beret who worked for the airlines in Phnom Penh. "You know, Jon, I have been a fighting man all my life," he says, "but I'm not built for this kind of stuff. I haven't cried since I was ten years old."

A Cambodian couple I know give away their seven-month-old baby, which will never survive the trip into the countryside. I am too choked to look them in the face. "He is my only baby. He is a beautiful baby," the wife says.

The Khmer Rouge will accept that a Cambodian woman married to a Frenchman under French law—and therefore possessing a French passport—has the right to stay with us. But there are many Frenchmen in the compound with Cambodian wives and children who do not have French passports, either because the wife had never bothered to apply, or because they had married in a Cambodian ceremony under Cambodian law. There are also many common-law wives. All of these the Khmer Rouge regard as Cambodians.

Now the "Big Boys" who sought asylum in the embassy leave too. These the Khmer Rouge really want, and they have come for them with guns in an army truck. There is Prince Sirik Matak, an architect of the coup against Sihanouk (his second cousin). He walks out the gate looking old, but erect. He knows he is probably going out to die. As he leaves he shakes a French gendarme's hand: "I am not afraid. I am ready to explain and to give account of what I have done."

"It is very sad, but we had to do it," says the consul, who turned the prince and the others out so as not to compromise our own chances of survival. "We are no longer men." And I see that he too is weeping.

8:20 p.m:

One of my colleagues, Jean-Jacques Cazaux, marries his Cambodian girlfriend, Thani Pho, twenty-five, to give her French nationality in the hope of saving her skin. The consul backdates the marriage to April 12 to trick the Khmer Rouge. It is fantastic. One man has got married, a woman has a new name, a baby was born in the compound this morning, a man died yesterday. We fete Cazaux's wedding with champagne and a Dundee cake. We don't feel the least bit guilty. Apparently they are eating turkey in the chancellery tonight and the Calmette doctors have a sideboard stacked with booze and food which they selfishly refuse to share. We label them *"Petits Francais"* and they hate us for it. Outside the atmosphere is sinister. Head-lamps ablaze, trucks of soldiers go up and down, searching for people hiding out in the city. Gunfire crashes in the suburbs. Today we are witnessing perhaps the deaths of thousands, the destruction of a way of life.

Monday, April 21:

Now the 150 Montagnards must leave the compound too. These people have fought for the Americans in Vietnam and Cambodia for ten years and this is the end of the road. Grimly they shoulder their pots and pans and bury their money and valuables. They harbour no illusions about the fate that awaits them. A mother screams over the four-year-old baby she must leave behind. She presses jewellery into our hands, and clasps us for comfort. Tears are running down all our cheeks. It is not a lack of bravery that has beaten them. They are a lost people and don't know what to do. A Frenchwoman sobs over her five Montagnard children and the husband she cannot follow. "My babies, my babies," she cries. Ragged, but so proud, the Montagnards move out.

Now Khmer Rouge soldiers with guns move in and search our compound. They look and poke and do not smile. They call up all remaining Asians to check their nationalities. They tell them they too must leave, then they change their minds. They are playing on our tattered nerves.

There are several key figures on which this community hangs. One is Doug Sapper, a great organizer and friend. He has a foul temper but he is a good, honest human being. He has lost everything in Cambodia, perhaps $100,000. Yet never once did I hear him complain. Another is the French archaeologist Francois Bizot who has lived in

Cambodia for eleven years. Bizot has lost his wife and entire family up the road. Publicly he has not shed a tear. He is one of those rare breed of men who thrive in adversity. He acts as a go-between with the Khmer Rouge and today he has talked them into letting him out. He returns with some pigs and water. If we get out of here alive we have much to thank him for. And, of course, there is Jean Dyrac, the consul, who knows what it is to suffer, having been a prisoner in World War II. He is intensely humble, a decent man whom the rough-and-tumble French *colons* here, who have lost all their worldly possessions, despise for his ponderous style. We owe him much.

And there are also those with whom we—who have abandoned our Cambodian friends—do not wish to pass the time of day. One is a twenty-four-year-old New Zealander and his Cambodian wife who, if she is lucky, will be able to stay. He is full of nauseating revolutionary rhetoric and extols the deeds of the "liberation forces." That they have kicked two million people out into the countryside without making adequate provision for feeding them, looted the city, ripped off watches, radios, cars, doesn't trouble his conscience a bit. "They are not looting, they are expropriating private property," he says. "The people give up their things willingly." But when it comes down to it he is as bourgeois and in need of his creature comforts as the rest of us. He is nearly always first in line for the food which we eat at 3:00 p.m.—a soggy mixture of rice mixed with a fragment of meat or vegetable, and he complains bitterly when the air conditioning stops. He also does little work. He and his wife, Chou Meng, fraternize with the Khmer Rouge guards over the walls. The more paranoid of us worry that they may be spies, passing on our little secrets. He has a low opinion of we members of the capitalist press and we of his hypocrisy. He is shunned.

3:30 p.m:

Jean Menta, Corsican adventurer (and, it is said, one time heroin smuggler) and the mercenary Borella, strangle and skin the embassy cat. The meat is tender like chicken.

Tuesday, April 22—10:30 a.m:

Life has suddenly got easier, presumably because the Cambodians we have been harbouring have left. The Khmer Rouge seem to be loosening up. They bring us water from the Mekong and pigs. Sapper kills the first, knocking it out with a neat axe blow, then slitting its throat with a jungle knife. Mike Daly uses his surgical skills to clean it. There are eighty-two kilos of meat for six hundred people. But tempers are frayed inside the compound. The squabbling over food is fantastic. Some people have a lot, some almost none, and the French *colons* accuse us "Internationals" of frivolity. They say we bathe naked in the rain (the only way to wash), dance and drink champagne and whisky galore. Would that it were true.

And there is increasing danger of disease. There are already more than one hundred cases of diarrhoea. Non-existent sanitation has turned this compound into a disagreeable collection of faeces. The *medicin-chef* of Calmette Hospital, Dr. Henri Revil, is constantly cabling Paris about the health problem. He exaggerates, of course, to convince Paris we must be sprung, but it is bad nevertheless. Someone is down with hepatitis, which is highly contagious.

5:20 p.m:

How gratifying to find that Khmer Rouge xenophobia encompasses their comrades of Eastern Europe too. They have expelled East German diplomat Erich Stange. We watch him climb down from his white embassy van, dishevelled and angry. Stange was on the last flight into Phnom Penh with me before the city's fall and I remember his enthusiasm for the imminent Communist victory and the bumbling of America. Now he runs over and shakes my hand. "I never expected this. We must have been mad to come back," he says. "How can they do this to me?"

He had several times refused to obey Khmer Rouge orders to quit his embassy. "But today," he says, "a Khmer Rouge with four pencils in his breast pocket—a colonel, I know these things by now—was very firm and gave us two hours to get out. I told him he knew very well that for five years East Germany has recognized his government, but he just shrugged. I understand. He is a peasant and behind him there is another one. There is no use to argue with such people."

Herr Stange is billeted with us. When he sees our room he is so downcast it is funny. We introduce him to his West German "countryman" Martin Bloecher. We tell him this is a workers' camp and he can work in the kitchen, sweep, dig latrines. He is not amused. But later tonight Stange is more affable, and chatters away with Bloecher.

Jean-Pierre, the French Maoist teacher, who has just arrived here after five voluntary days with Khmer Rouge forces in the countryside, says the Khmer Rouge have sealed off each section of the city for searching. They do not take risks but fire grenades and B40 rockets into buildings where they think snipers may still be hidden. If they cannot search a building or street efficiently they burn it down with incendiary grenades.

Wednesday, April 23—9:30 a.m:

Smiling Khmer Rouge officials deliver six bottles of Johnny Walker, brandy and cigarettes. These peasant folks are getting a feeling for our decadent Western tastes.

One thing is clear, that there is no political government yet in Phnom Penh and that there may not be for months. The military are firmly in charge and perhaps the struggle for power is not yet over. They are keeping the politicians out. There is clearly a clash of opinions on the fundamental aims of the revolution between the military inside the country and the political facade outside. The Khmer Rouge we have seen do not deny the existence of Sihanouk's Royal Government of National Opinion (GRUNK) but they have used him and it for diplomatic purposes only. Their revolution is total. There is no room for compromise. The Khmer Rouge are abandoning everything connected with the defeated regime. They have no time for cities, which in their eyes are parasites living off the sweat of the peasants. This is why they have evacuated Phnom Penh. Salvation lies in the fields and it is to the fields that they have sent the city's people. It is a sweeping, unprecedented reform, brutal in its application, but for the sake of the Cambodian people who have suffered so much one can only hope it will work. At least the country is now at peace.

Thursday, April 24:

Jean Remy, head of the French Planters' Association, and Cambodia's most influential Frenchman, is here after a week on the roads. He says he hears the Khmer Rouge are executing army officers at the rubber nurseries in the suburbs.

9:30 a.m:

Wild cheering in the compound as a Chinese four-engine jet passes overhead and lands at the airport which we assumed was out of order. We speculate whether it brings Cambodian and Chinese officials from Peking or Hanoi and hope it will take us out.

Our confinement is causing fits of depression and we quarrel over trifling things. People get strange obsessions under forced confinement. Photographer Denis Cameron, who stayed behind to try to arrange the evacuation of five hundred orphans to Australia, sits morosely in his corner obsessively killing flies with a fly spray. Even Al Rockoff, the multi-wounded combat photographer who finds the spray chokes his lungs and sends him into dangerous coughing fits, cannot dissuade him.

"You are going to die," we joke with the coughing Rockoff, remembering how his heart had stopped when he was last wounded a year ago and how a Swedish nurse had pummelled his chest and revived him.

He gives his usual reply: "Well, it won't be for the first time."

Tuesday, April 29—7:20 p.m:

Tomorrow six hundred of us are leaving by road for the Thai border. The Khmer Rouge announced this outrageous evacuation plan on Saturday at the end of a three-day special National Congress which said Cambodia's new rulers will countenance no foreign interference, either military or humanitarian. I am sure the thousands of hungry people up the road, who have relied on international relief agencies for several years, will be interested to hear this.

I say outrageous because, of course, it would be so simple for us to fly out now that the airport is open and that a French transport plane is on stand-by at Vientiane. But, of course, to try to probe the Khmer Rouge mind is fruitless. To apply Western logic to it is an irrelevance. I don't think they are being bloody-minded. It's just that they have no faith in planes, and who can blame them? The only ones they know were American and those bombed them. The United States has much to answer for here, not only in terms of human lives and massive material destruction. The rigidity and nastiness of the un-Cambodian-like fellows who run this country now, or what is left of it, are as much a product of this wholesale American bombing which has hardened and honed their minds as they are a product of Marx and Mao.

Choosing who should be on the first evacuation convoy has caused incredible unpleasantness. I am sorry to say some of my colleagues have dubbed as "cowards" we six journalists whom the consul wants to go out first to try to organize an embargo on events here till everyone is out. We try to placate them with the last of the champagne, but bitterness persists.

Today has been especially trying. The Khmer Rouge, once more showing an amazing ability to turn nasty at any time, suddenly announce that no Asian without papers can leave. This means the splitting up of more families, including West German Martin Bloecher's, whose Thai wife does not have a passport yet, and the New Zealand revolutionary and his Cambodian wife. There have been tearful, emotional scenes. Fear, apprehension, panic are once more written on people's faces.

Wednesday, April 30:

By accident or design, the Khmer Rouge's convoy of twenty-six lorries took us out of Phnom Penh on a circuitous route that avoided travel on Highway Five, the main axis of the population's exodus.

Five years ago, the Phnom Penh we left behind was one of the loveliest cities in South East Asia. It was not only the old French colonial architecture, the glittering pagodas, that gave it its enchantment, it was the warmth and grace of its people. Now the people have gone and Phnom Penh, as we drive through the suburbs, is a sinister wasteland. Every single building in the city has been turned upside down in the soldiers' search for food and booty—from the Russian Embassy where they stamped on Mr. Brezhnev's picture and fired a B40 rocket through the window, to the stilted houses of the poor on the outskirts. They have wrecked the city's water plant and shut down all of its factories.

The empty, dustblown streets were lined with hundreds of abandoned cars and motor-bikes, cannibalized by the Khmer Rouge, their tires cut to make Ho Chi Minh sandals. We passed whole districts gutted by fire, with hungry pigs and dogs rooting through the ruins for scraps. The Khmer Rouge's army, now the city's only occupants, has shown little pride in its prize. The main attraction to these country boys, who fought and won a war against a corrupt, American-backed regime, has been the multitude of watches, radios and trinkets they have been able to loot from shops.

The road out of the city, past the airport, was lined with abandoned property, evidence of the hurried migration—a giant boneyard of everything from trucks and cars to helmets, uniforms and TV sets. The rotting vehicles continued for miles, abandoned as the petrol ran out. Some drivers, angry at the thought of leaving what was probably their pride and joy to the Khmer Rouge, had pushed them into pools of stagnant water. Motorized transport in Cambodia is now almost non-existent. We were to see no more than a half-dozen moving vehicles in our 260-mile journey. They were driven by Khmer Rouge officers, and badly too.

The mind still gropes at the horror and enormity of the emptying of Phnom Penh. But has there been a "bloodbath" in the city in the more conventional style of military revenge? The American diplomats here used to assure us that the revenge would be dreadful when the Khmer

Rouge came. I can only say that what I have seen and heard provides no proof of a bloodbath. My overriding impression—reinforced as we journeyed through the countryside en route to the Thai border—was that the Khmer Rouge military authorities had ordered this mass evacuation not to *punish* the people but to *revolutionalize* their ways and thoughts. Many thousands will no doubt die. But whatever else, this does not constitute a deliberate campaign of terror, rather it points to poor organization, lack of vision and the brutalization of a people by a long and savage war.

Thursday, May 1:

It took two bone-jarring days to travel the first eighty miles because of the appalling condition of the roads and the bad organization of our guides. Our journey is so slow. We lose our way and have to backtrack and the frustration grows as we find ourselves passing the same spot where we were twelve hours before. Then two trucks break down and after yet another long delay, we are only able to get moving again by towing one of them. Much of our progress over the bomb-damaged roads is at less than five miles per hour.

We have come to an even more startling realization: that outside Phnom Penh virtually every other city, town, village and hamlet that resisted the Communists has also been emptied out into the countryside. The greater part of this nation of seven million, which has endured one of the most savage, futile wars of modern times, has been uprooted, its people hungry and bewildered.

Tonight we reached the provincial capital of Kompong Chhnang and found it emptied of its 500,000 people. In the nearby countryside we had the opportunity to say a few fleeting words with a male nurse, Tong San, from Kompong Chhnang Hospital (he was recognized by the Scottish medical team who had trained him). He said that on April 20, Khmer Rouge carried away all the hospital patients in lorries and dumped them eighteen miles in the forest without food or water. For ten days now Tong San has been wandering aimlessly. The Khmer Rouge have given nobody firm instructions as to where to go or what to do. They only tell them to keep on moving. "We are lost and confused," he said. "The Khmer Rouge do not accept money so I exchange my clothes for rice to eat."

We met Tong San in a long-established Khmer Rouge collective village a few miles outside Kompong Chhnang. The villagers seemed a dull, uninspiring lot. Doubtless they are every bit as hardworking as the peasant of old, but somehow they lack his bounce. Everyone wears black, and the women universally have Maoist haircuts. One of the marvellous things about Cambodia used to be the spontaneity and gaiety of its people, even towards strangers. Now a wave and a smile is returned by wooden stares.

The war damage here, as everywhere else we saw, is total. Not a bridge is standing, hardly a house. I am told most villagers spent the war years living semi-permanently underground in earth bunkers to escape the bombing. Little wonder that this peasant army is proud of its achievements. Sitting down with me to a meal of boiled rice and meat from a freshly killed pig, the local chief said: "I and my men worked in the fields during the day and fought at night. That was how we won."

The whole countryside has been churned up by American B-52 bomb craters, whole towns and villages razed. So far I have not seen one intact pagoda. Yet the monks are still there, though now in fewer numbers than before, showing that they have at least been tolerated by the Communists.

At one village we passed—on the day we left Phnom Penh—where part of a 500-pound American bomb still hangs from a tree as an air raid signalling gong, the villagers told us proudly they harvested three crops of rice a year. These particular villagers were among the very few friendly people we saw during our trip. They had a generous sense of hospitality, feeding us before they ate themselves, and it was regrettable that we made a sordid spectacle of ourselves, stampeding for their food, breaking plates, tipping over bowls of rice and stealing their coconuts in our haste to eat. Our wild behaviour surely hardened the Khmer Rouge's conviction that we Westerners have no business in their new society and are better out of Cambodia altogether.

It is ironic that throughout this exhausting ride, some of the greediest, most selfish among us were the Russian diplomats and their wives. While the rest of us nibbled on the odd Red Cross biscuit and a handful of rice, they settled down of an evening to a four-course meal of food brought along with their personal possessions, washed down with vodka and tea. Not satisfied, they had the gall to demand their portion of the communal food. Nor did they share their meals with a Bulgarian woman who was in the same lorry, claiming she was our responsibility. As the chorus of protests rose the Russians threatened to expose those Westerners who, with the connivance of Francois Bizot, the French diplomat, had smuggled aboard two or three Cambodian women who had been forbidden to leave the country. Only when we journalists threatened to splash their names in the world's press, expose their bourgeois tastes and refusal to feed one of their Warsaw Pact allies, did they relent. Today we were delighted to receive a placatory bottle of vodka.

Among those whom Monsieur Bizot smuggled aboard,

incidentally, was the wife of the revolutionary New Zealand student. At the last minute Bizot pushed the weeping couple into a truck behind the backs of the guards. Perhaps they now have a taste of what revolution is all about.

Friday, May 2:

Last night was the lowest spot of this arduous journey. While our guides tried to find us somewhere to sleep we sat for four hours in the open lorries in a driving rainstorm. We slept finally on the stone floor of the magistrates' court in Kompong Chhnang. During the night a nine-month-old baby died of exposure.

As we approached the next town, Pursat, came potentially the most dangerous incident of our trip. The convoy was stopped by a group of Khmer Rouge soldiers who demanded that we hand over the Americans on board. We managed to bluff it through. Otherwise the knots of Khmer Rouge soldiers we passed showed little interest in our presence.

Saturday, May 3:

The journey is almost over by now and the vice-consul, Monsieur Morin, and the United Nations and Red Cross officials stop the convoy a few miles short of the border. They go down to a river and shave and bathe. Is this a bad joke? There are sick and hungry people on this convoy waiting for the border. These people are delaying them because they want to make themselves unreal.

At last we reach the safety of the Thai border after our gruelling 260-mile ride. We journalists had agreed to honour the embargo on news until the entire group of "Internationals" had reached safety. During the week we have time to take stock.

Much has been written in the newspapers that reflects

the new Cambodia in an unfavourable light. After the sorrows I have seen I am certainly no apologist for the excesses of the new regime, but I feel it would be wrong to condemn a whole nation and its chances of a decent, peaceful future on the terrible things that have happened over these past weeks.

In the last five years Cambodia has lost upwards of half a million people, 10 per cent of its population, in a war fuelled and waged on its soil by outside powers for their own selfish reasons. The people who run, live in and try to reconstruct the heap of ruins they have inherited in Cambodia today deserve the world's compassion and understanding.

The Sunday Times, London
May 11, 1975

VI

A Million Dead is a Statistic

IN THE SPRING OF 1976, I went back as close as I could get to Cambodia. The war had been over for a year. Cambodia was the Democratic Republic of Kampuchea. The phantoms of the jungle were in control. (They, in turn, have since been deposed.) Pathetic refugees were scrambling into Thailand, starving and shot at, separated from their families, flooding the primitive refugee camps with a horrible human mess.

I took Marie with me to the border of Thailand at Aranyaprathet. I shouldn't have because bandits hit fairly frequently along the two hundred miles of highway from Bangkok. But women who are stuck on the rock of Hong Kong for long periods of time seem to suffer a form of claustrophobia and I had thought Marie would agree to remain in Bangkok to buy silks and teapots. She didn't agree and she came.

In the circumstances I checked more carefully than usual, with Peter Collins of CBS and other staff correspondents in Bangkok, on the state of the road. We delayed departure for a day until Mike, the driver of car number five at the Oriental Hotel, who had been highly recommended by Tony Paul, was available. It is an essential part of the art, any experienced foreign correspondent will tell a new chum, to pick a driver who is more scared than you are. This is one of the better guarantees of survival. Mike was suitably and sensibly scared.

The suitably-scared driver is not concerned much for your safety, of course. You are just a rich nut who wants to go where no sane person would want to go, and your stupidity is such that you deserve to be killed. He is scared for his own safety, but more importantly for his car, usually an American model of early 1960s vintage, held together by loving care and bits of wire. This is his lifetime investment and the precious support of his family.

Some drivers in Vietnam, like Hughie, whom I shared with the CBC, had an amazing instinct for survival. Acting on some strange intuition he would pull his old rattletrap off the road and dive into a ditch minutes before a shell exploded anywhere near his source of livelihood, himself and incidentally us.

Only in Beirut, which sent veteran Vietnam correspondents back to Hong Kong heaving huge sighs of relief, and which mercifully I covered only briefly during the 1978 Israeli invasion, did the scared-driver rule not apply, and possibly for good reason. In that crazily inhumane mess of hate and rubble, the drivers were often so scared they couldn't function properly at all. They had to be threatened and bullied. The excessive amount of fear some of them exuded was offensive, making the car an unpleasant place. The journey "up the road" was unduly dangerous because the correspondent had to use his own judgment almost entirely.

Mike, the scared, proud owner-driver of car number five, took us to Aranyaprathet without incident. He even played soft, European classical music on a stereo system, either to soothe himself or us as he picked up speed through the bush-lined sections of the highway where the bandits usually hid. He introduced us to the only restaurant in Aranyaprathet with its only non-rice dish of tough chicken legs, and he booked us into a complex of cottages on the edge of the village. The toilet was a plastic bucket and a hole in the floor but the cottage was clean.

There were about three thousand refugees in a camp on the fringes of Aranyaprathet, not far from the border crossing at Poipet. They were surviving on a ration of two cans of rice a day and a little fish or meat every three days. Big families huddled in tiny squalid spaces behind barbed wire. There was no water supply, but the refugees were allowed to walk once a day to a river about half a mile away to carry water in kerosene cans.

Marie and I were not allowed inside the camp, although some Christian missionaries were. They were distributing T-shirts marked "Jesus Saves" to the Buddhist inmates. Mike, the driver, was allowed to go in and he brought a selection of Cambodians to the guarded gate to meet us.

Korm Kery, fifty-two, the first man who came, couldn't shake hands because his were covered in festering sores, and he could hardly walk because he had been shot three times while escaping. My notes show that he said:

I am a major. I was one of the senior officers in the camp at Battambang when Phnom Penh fell on April 17.
After we surrendered we were put in a school and

97

guarded, of course. On April 22 at 2 p.m. the Khmer Rouge came and said senior officers were to go to Phnom Penh to welcome Prince Sihanouk. We were told to collect our clothes, uniforms and whatever food we had.

At 2:30 p.m. we were told to get into trucks. There were six trucks and a bus. There were 312 of us. We drove in a convoy with the Khmer Rouge in a jeep and a Land Rover escorting us about twenty kilometres from Battambang. The convoy turned off the road to Phnom Penh toward a mountain called Tipbodia.

About two hundred metres from the foot of the mountain they told us to get off the trucks and rest, and the trucks drove away. Then we realized there was going to be the executions of all of us.

Another officer and I ran into the jungle. They fired at us and I was wounded in the arm. There was the sound of guns behind us, machine guns and rifles. The Khmer Rouge were firing from west to east and east to west. The other officers were all caught in the crossfire. I saw them fall down. Then there was just smoke.

We hid for two nights in the jungle then I went back to Battambang to look for my family. I have, or I had, thirteen children aged between two-and-a-half and twenty-four. I hid for three days and nights in a temple and tried to make contact with them, but I learned they had been ordered to leave Battambang.

I ran at night to another village where I pretended I had never been a soldier. I was sent to work in the fields growing rice until February, when I heard five ex-soldiers had been caught and shot.

A lot of people were dying, hundreds of them, and I was sick too, so I was taken to hospital for three days. Then I said I was well enough to go back to work but I escaped into the jungle.

*I moved at night through the jungle for twelve days. I
didn't have anything to eat except roots and leaves. Then
when I got near the border they saw me and fired at me. I
was shot in the back, an arm and a leg. I was all covered
in blood, but I crawled over the border.*

*I am not well now, but I would like to go back to try to
find my family again. I suppose most of them are dead.*

*Would you tell the free world that Cambodia needs
help?*

Marie went to the village and bought some strep-
tomycin for the major's festering sores. He was very
grateful.

One by one Mike brought more men to the camp gate.
Thi Campa-Het was a tough-looking, shy man of twenty-
nine, who had been a private in the Cambodian army for a
year before Phnom Penh fell. When we talked to him, two
months after he escaped to Thailand, he still had deep
rope burns on his arms. Thi said:

*I come from the village of Tuktala, near Sisophon in the
northwest. When the Khmer Rouge came I did not say I
was a soldier. I spent eight months growing rice.*

*Then, on January 3, the Khmer Rouge put me in jail
with about a hundred others. They must have discovered I
had been a soldier. I was three days in the jail. They tied
our legs with chains, two or three men on each length of
chain.*

*One January 7 they said they were taking us out to
grow rice again and they put us into trucks, but they tied
our legs with ropes and they bound our arms behind our
backs with red nylon rope, which is the sign of death.*

*There were forty-eight people in the truck I was in and
we were driven down Route 5 to a mountain near Poipet.*

The men in the truck started crying because they knew what was going to happen.

Near a temple near the mountain some of the Khmer Rouge, five of them, got off the truck and started to walk behind. I managed to get my legs a bit loose and a man in front of me got his arms completely untied. I signalled to him that I was sitting on an iron bar and to hit the one Khmer Rouge still on the truck with it.

He hit the Khmer Rouge on the head with the iron bar and we both jumped off the truck and crawled into the jungle. I got my feet loose and was able to run. They shot at me but missed. I ran about a hundred metres, lay down, and looked back to see what the Khmer Rouge was doing. I could not see for the smoke but many guns were firing and people were crying and screaming.

Gradually over two days, as Mike brought out more and more refugees, the horrible enormity of the story of Cambodia after the war unfolded. The refugees told of an occurrence, perhaps without precedence in history, of a whole country turned into a giant, moving *gulag*; of a people terrorized and driven into unpaid work gangs; families purposely split, denied food and sex, moving across the country to whatever labour was required, dying on the roads from exhaustion or execution, dropping dead from disease or starvation in the paddy fields.

They drew a picture of a strange new society, run by the former phantoms of the jungle, now known mysteriously as the *Angka Loeu*—the Organization on High. It was the society that Swain had seen developing even as Phnom Penh fell; one that had no monetary system, no schools, transportation, telephones, electricity, shops, private property; only the long lines of forced, unpaid labour in the paddy fields and death for the weak, the educated and the ideologically incompatible. It was no less than an attempt to create a new man, faithful to the thoughts of the Organization on High, by killing the old and the unconvertible, often with clubs because bullets were scarce. It was genocide; enormous and ugly and unknown to the rest of the world.

A US State Department specialist, Kenneth M. Quinn, had written with remarkable perception in 1974 that the Communist Khmer Rouge had committed themselves to "total social revolution which would be accomplished by psychologically reconstructing individual members of society."

This process [he wrote] *entails stripping away, through terror and other means, the traditional bases, structures and forces which have shaped and guided an individual's life until he is left as an atomized, isolated unit; and then rebuilding him according to party doctrine by substituting a series of new values, organizations and ethical norms.*

Nobody at the time, of course, believed such nonsense. But we did, as I interviewed the refugees at Aranyaprathet and Marie shuttled back and forth from the village bringing more antibiotics for the open sores and rotting limbs of the lucky survivors.

Part of the story of the cruel, complete evacuation of Phnom Penh, and of all the other cities of Cambodia, was told by Swain and the few other correspondents who stayed to cover the Khmer Rouge victory and saw the start of the evacuation from their refuge in the French Embassy. But the full story was not known until these surviving dregs of the disaster began to talk in the Thai refugee camps. After hundreds of similar interviews, before and after mine, mainly in the camp of Aranyaprathet, Tony Paul and John

Barron pieced the terrible evacuation story together and wrote in their book, *Murder of a Gentle Land*:

Inexplicably, the Communists concentrated initially upon expelling the sick and wounded from hospitals which were jammed with fresh casualties of the last bombardment. Troops stormed into the Preah Ket Melea Hospital, Phnom Penh's largest and oldest, and shouted to patients, physicians and nurses alike, "Out! Everybody out! Get out!" They made no distinction between bedridden and ambulatory patients, between the convalescing and the dying, between those awaiting surgery and those who had just undergone surgery. Hundreds of men, women and children in pajamas limped, hobbled, struggled out of the hospital into the streets where the midday sun had raised the temperature to well over 100 degrees Fahrenheit. Relatives or friends pushed the beds of patients too wounded, crippled or enfeebled to walk, some holding aloft perfusion bottles dripping plasma or serum into the bodies of loved ones. One man carried his son, whose legs had just been amputated. The bandages on both stumps were red with blood, and the son, who appeared to be about twenty-two, was screaming, "You can't leave me like this! Kill me! Please kill me!"

Ang Sokthan, twenty-two, was a pharmacy student at the University of Phnom Penh when the city fell. She was a pretty girl, but painfully thin when I interviewed her in Aranyaprathet. Sometimes as we talked, she tried to smile, but she couldn't make it. Instead, tears welled into her big brown eyes. This is her story:

On the day Phnom Penh fell, at about 5 p.m. some Khmer Rouge soldiers came to our house and told us we would have to leave the city because the United States was going to come back and bomb it. Our parents were not in Phnom Penh, so I walked with my brother Savin, who was twenty-six, an engineer, my brother Sokun, who was twenty-four, a student in electronics, and my sister Sokphal, who was twenty, a high school student, until we were about a kilometre from the outskirts of the city.

There were thousands of people on the road and dead people beside it. We were very tired so we stayed the night in a temple and in the morning we marched again. We walked for another three days and then asked the Khmer Rouge if we could rest because one of the other women we had met on the way was having a baby. They let us rest for a while.

It was very terrible. We had no food at all and we had walked for three days and three nights. They let us stop for a while at a village called Batheby about forty kilometres from Phnom Penh.

Next day my sister and I were made to walk across the rice paddies for about ten kilometres and put to work making a dam. We had never done any manual work before and our job was to carry heavy loads of soil in baskets to make a dam.

We did this for three months, working 5 a.m. to 10:30 p.m., and sometimes longer on nights when the moon was out. It was very terrible. Even if it was raining we had to keep on working.

At first we were given a small tin can and a half of rice per person per day, but after a month the rice ran out and we were fed little bits of corn. After another month all we got was berries. People were very sick. When they fainted from hunger or malaria they were taken back to the village. We slept in a tent and we were very unhappy. We had no soap to clean ourselves. I lost a lot of weight.

After three months, one morning at 1 a.m., the Khmer Rouge said all the people working on the dam would have to move to another village. We walked a long way through the night and were taken by truck to a station and then by train to Sisophon, near the Thai border. There was no food or water on the train, but we met our brothers who had been working the rice paddies and were very sick from starvation and malaria. My brothers were taken to a hospital in a school. It was filthy. There was just one potion kept in used penicillin bottles and given to all patients no matter what was wrong with them. Most of the "doctors" and other hospital staff were illiterate.

My sister and I were sent out to make another dam, but this time we had to work waist-deep in the water. We got only half a can of rice a day and sometimes two extra cans of unhusked rice. After a while the Khmer Rouge came and told us our brothers were seriously sick and we could go to the hospital to look after them.

The hospital had one "doctor" then and was full of people with diarrhoea and malaria and people with swollen bodies from malnutrition. A lot of them were dying, dozens of them. My brother Savin died first and then my brother Sokun a week later. They were buried in a field without any ceremony or anything, just as if they were animals.

I decided then it was best to die quickly by a bullet rather than slowly like all the other people. So, soon after that—it was in November—my sister and I escaped from Sisophon with thirty others. We walked for three nights toward the border until I couldn't walk any farther. My foot was cut by thorns and I kept falling down. I told my sister and a man who was with us to go ahead and I lay down in the jungle to die. But I felt better after a while and wandered by myself in the jungle following the sun for eight days without anything to eat. I licked dew from leaves to try to stop the thirst.

On the ninth morning I woke up near a cow trail by a village. I hoped it was in Thailand. There were two men on the trail and I ran out, grabbed the older man by the hand and said, "I've just escaped from Cambodia!" The younger man asked, "Is she human?" He spoke in Thai; I knew I was free.

Only eight of the thirty who set out from Sisophon got across the border. Some of them told me my sister must have died near the border. They said they had heard an explosion or gunshot and had found a dead girl.

I was very sick but I feel better now.

She tried to smile again, but she couldn't.

The stories poured out as Mike brought the pathetic, lucky refugees to the gate: Bodies rotting on the roadsides or thrown into rivers, ruining the drinking water. Young women, probably prostitutes, bludgeoned to death with blows to the back of the head. Bodies of children, one every two hundred yards on some parts of some roadways, dead from dehydration. Loved ones hacked to death with hoes. A large group of women on a cart track east of Khal Kabei, buried up to their necks, their throats stabbed, their heads swollen with putrefaction.

At that time, in the spring of 1976, a year after the fall of Phnom Penh, I made a rough, very unscientific guess at the number killed in the genocide. I simply subtracted from the total population of Cambodia (which had been more than seven million) the 20 to 30 per cent that those I interviewed said they knew to have been executed or died from disease or starvation. I wrote a story stating there were more than a million dead.

"Was it Stalin," Marie asked sadly as I was pounding the typewriter, "who said a single death is a tragedy but a million deaths is a statistic?"

Anthony Paul and John Barron, after much more careful research, estimated that 1.2 million men, women, and children died in Cambodia between April 17, 1975, and December 1976, as a consequence of the actions of the *Angka Loeu*. Father François Ponchaud, a priest who had originally been a Khmer Rouge sympathizer, interviewed thousands of refugees after his escape from Phnom Penh. He put the figure at closer to two million.

But the world didn't care much. In North America, foreign coverage was concentrated on the Middle East and Africa. A few countries, Britain, America, Canada, and Norway, kicked up a bit of a fuss at the United Nations Human Rights Commission. Amnesty International asked for an investigation, and a few organizations and individuals in the Western world reacted with shock and horror. But in general the crimes of the Organization on High rated only a few paragraphs every now and again in the papers.

The People's Republic of Kampuchea was a tightly closed country so the TV cameras couldn't take pictures. In the new media era, if there aren't any pictures, stories don't get on the TV newscasts, so they just don't happen. And the world was sick and tired of the troubles of Southeast Asia and Indochina anyway.

After we had done dozens of interviews at the refugee camp, we drove to the bridge at Poipet, the tumble-down metal and wood structure that separated Thailand from Cambodia. From the Thai side we could see black-suited Khmer Rouge soldiers a few hundred yards away unloading crates of liquor from US Army trucks. Thais on motorcycles and on foot were moving on trails through the jungle, apparently using another crossing of the narrow river which we couldn't see. They were carrying gasoline in every kind of container imaginable—from bottles and jugs to kerosene cans and oil drums—into Cambodia, and returning with cases of bottles of good French wine and Johnny Walker Red Label Scotch.

I fitted a 200-millimetre lens to my Nikon and walked along the bridge to take pictures of this operation and especially of the Khmer Rouge soldiers. Mike and Marie yelled at me to come back and they hid behind a concrete bridge pylon. Through the long distance lens I could see the Khmer soldiers aiming rifles at me. But they didn't shoot.

For some personal, emotional reason I wanted to defy this new man, these automats created by the Organization of High in the land that used to be so lovely. So I continued to walk until I was just more than halfway across the bridge, clicking the camera, watching the men in the black pajamas run and hide from the little lens that could turn the eyes of the outside world upon them and their ignorance. They ran behind bushes and posts and trucks and raised their rifles, but they didn't fire.

It was a stupid, unprofessional thing to do. They were too far away even for the long distance lens. I knew the pictures wouldn't be much good and eventually the paper didn't use them. But for some reason, as I walked back across the bridge into Thailand, I felt better.

"You're crazy, sir," Mike said gently when I was safely back on solid Thai soil, and he hustled me quickly into his car.

VII

Flight from Danang

IN THE CENTRAL HIGHLANDS AND northern provinces of South Vietnam more than a million people took to the roads early in 1975, some for the third or fourth time, pushing their pathetically-few worldly possessions on carts or on bikes southward, in one of history's great exoduses.

Their panic was contagious and cumulative. Some said they abandoned their towns and villages because they feared they would be killed by the Communists. Some told us they left because government officials had told them to leave. Most of them said they left simply because everybody else was leaving in a panic. Not one of the hundreds I talked to said they had left because of a love of freedom or because of loyalty to the constitutional government of President Thieu. And not all of them fled. In the two-thirds of the country already controlled by the Communists at least six of the eight million people remained, giving some credence to the Communists' claim that they commanded the loyalty of the majority of the people.

But those who did flee left towns and villages simultaneously undefended and unconquered, with the retreat outpacing the offensive by many days, so the streets of the towns were eerily empty and silent. The refugees clogged the narrow roads to the coast in an endless pathetic procession we called the "Trail of Tears." They became, those who survived, the first of the "boat people," who continued the exodus in leaky craft. They either drowned or scattered themselves on the coasts of Thailand, Malaysia, Indonesia, and even far away Australia, where they were virtually forgotten for almost five years. Then the richer, more sophisticated, ethnic Chinese community of Vietnam began their more visible flight in bigger boats. The TV cameras were able to capture the escapes of the more publicity-conscious Chinese. Space for their stories suddenly became available in the newspapers. Statistics were transformed into real people and belatedly the world began to care.

The correspondents based in Saigon knew the war was over when the northern imperial capital of Hue, the spiritual centre of the country, with its emperors' tombs, fell without a fight on March 26, 1975. This created yet another exodus of civilians, but mainly of soldiers, abandoning their weapons, shoving civilians aside on the roads. They scrambled for boats, under contemptuous Communist fire, to take them down the coast to Danang, the second biggest city of South Vietnam.

Hue fell so suddenly it caught all of us in the comparative comfort of Saigon or out on the coastal roads with the earlier refugees, so that one of the biggest stories of the Vietnam War was virtually uncovered. Peter Arnett, of Associated Press, the old pro who won a Pulitzer Prize for his war coverage, made an attempt to get in to Hue from Danang with two Vietnamese NBC cameramen, but their jeep could not move against the stream of refugees pouring through the Hai Van Pass not far from Danang. Anyway, the bridges on the road were blown away so they had to turn back. Paul Vogle, the skinny, affable, hard-drinking correspondent of UPI, who speaks perfect Vietnamese, managed to talk his way onto a rescue helicopter and landed in Hue briefly to record some of the panicky evacuation scene, but that was all.

And it was not easy to get into Danang. The Air Vietnam commercial flights out of the city were naturally packed with richer refugees, and for some inexplicable reason the flights in were also booked for days ahead. It was too far and too dangerous to travel by road. In the circumstances, the lonely newspaper journalist, who has no logistical backup and no funds to charter planes or choppers, has to call in a few debts. ABC owed me a few for "pigeoning" film out of Cambodia or somewhere. I had forgotten where, but their crews remembered, and in their cluttered Saigon bureau headquarters, a room at the Caravelle Hotel, we made a deal.

They had chartered a plane to deliver film to a cameraman in Nha Trang, halfway up the coast to Danang, but the pilot was scared and unreliable. His old aircraft had two engines but it was also unreliable, they pointed out. But if I would make sure their ABC film was delivered at Nha Trang, I could take the plane on to Danang, provided, of course, the pilot would go on.

The pigeoning system was one of the nicer things about covering the wars, where correspondents lived and worked together in difficult circumstances. The competition, particularly between the TV networks and the wire services, was always intense, but there was a general understanding that anybody moving toward any efficient communications facility would carry and file anybody else's film or stories.

In Phnom Penh there was even an official pigeon roster, essentially for the wire services and TV networks, for running the gauntlet of rockets pounding the airport. A correspondent for an individual newspaper could repay some of the debts he owed for transportation and protection by the TV crews, or for access to the wire services copy, by volunteering to take his turn carrying the daily bundle to a departing aircraft.

Once, in Saigon, I heard that CBS was chartering an Air Vietnam 707 jet to fly a single bag of film to Hong Kong. I heard about it because the CBS crews were highly and vocally annoyed about the fact that the government airline would charter only its luxury jet, with a full first-class crew and extra stewardesses, at an additional cost of several thousand dollars.

"No use wasting all that space," I told the CBS bureau chief, Brian Ellis, who was a good friend. "I've got a roll of film that has to get to Toronto." So my single little Kodak cassette won the only other occupied seat on the large plane to Hong Kong, where the CBS staff shipped it immediately to Toronto. The pictures were in the paper less than twenty-four hours after I had taken them.

But when I arrived at Than Son Nhut airport to board the ABC's charter to Nha Trang and on to Danang it was difficult to believe that my past efforts at pigeoning had paid off this time. The small monoplane was at least forty years old. One wing appeared to be attached to the fuselage with what looked like old, unbent, coat hangers. The pilot was at least sixty, probably sixty-five years old. He peered at his charts from about an inch away, as if he was almost blind. And he spoke only French. I had been wondering why Jim Bennett, the toughest of the ABC correspondents, who was himself trying to get into Danang, had not taken advantage of this ABC charter. As I

climbed into the cockpit beside the ancient pilot, the reason dawned on me. Bennett was a survivor.

We got off the ground, however, taking up an amazing
amount of Tan Son Nhut's long runway in the process. We
arrived in Nha Trang and assumed that we had delivered
the film for ABC. Helicopters were landing at the airport,
disgorging unarmed soldiers and a few civilians from the
Trail of Tears. But the terminal buildings were ghostly
quiet and the parts of the once-beautiful seaside city we
could see appeared to have been abandoned. The old pilot
opened doors and shouted at each of the airport's empty
buildings until finally a Vietnamese emerged from one of
them and agreed to accept the film.

The Vietnamese man said he knew where the stringer
was, although he seemed to me to be confused about
whether the man worked for ABC or NBC. In any event he
knew a television cameraman who probably needed film
and this was good enough for the old French pilot. When I
tried to argue that we should personally deliver the film,
he climbed into his funny old plane and revved its engines
ominously. He did agree to fly on to Danang, though, over
beaches on which small groups of refugees huddled, skirt-
ing carefully around the black smoke from several artillery
battles. But when we were over Danang he talked briefly
with the control tower and refused to land.

I shouted at him in English: "Put the thing down, you
old bastard. You're going to have to get gas anyway."

"*La guerre est là*," he shouted back. "*Impossible.*"

The runway looked peaceful and empty enough so I
grabbed the control column and pushed it forward. I was
stronger than he was so he landed the thing. He didn't
bother about gas. He didn't even cut his engine. He was
supposed to wait for me but as soon as I stepped onto the

tarmac he took off. It was lonely standing in the centre of the big, empty tarmac, but I was glad he was gone.

Jim Bennett was in the terminal, having somehow wangled a place on a commercial flight with two other American correspondents who had chartered a plane. Peter Arnett had returned to Danang after his unsuccessful attempt to get into Hue and he and Bruce Wilson of the Melbourne *Herald* were trying to get out. They briefed us innocents on the events of the last few hours.

Hue had completely collapsed and the refugees and routed soldiers were pouring into downtown Danang. There were rumours that some of the leaders of the First Infantry Division had been killed when a helicopter was shot down just south of the city. A rocket attack on the air base had killed six people and wounded thirty-four in the slums on the base's periphery.

Arnett, the most experienced of the Vietnam correspondents, who had long since earned his epaulets for courage and wisdom, told me: "This is no place to be, Jack. It's time to get out. The war is over, up here at least."

But we couldn't get out. Arnett, Wilson and a TV crew had the last seats on the last plane. It was hot and the terminal was packed with the leftovers from this last flight out, but the stall selling the usual warm beer with a chunk of filthy ice was still open. I found a space at a table and rattled off the story as Wilson had told it to me while I drank three dirty, cooling beers. Wilson almost missed the plane in his wait to pigeon out for me what was really his own story.

Bennett's local Vietnamese crew had a jeep so the four of us who were left behind drove downtown and checked in to the Grande Hotel on the waterfront. There were huge crowds of refugees on the docks. Dishevelled, obviously completely-demoralized soldiers were pouring ashore from big landing barges, sometimes pushing the civilians aside. There was no panic and not much noise except for the occasional sound of a three-wheeled Lambretta bus, disgorging more refugees, with their most precious possessions, their sewing machines, radios, baskets of fruit and rice. Mostly there was a strange, dazed silence in downtown Danang, and we were the only guests at the Grande Hotel.

We had just checked in when John Swenson, of the US Information Service, told us to check out again. "Full evacuation," he said. "Everybody out including newsmen. I don't know how you got here, but you've got to go. We'll have a plane in to take you out tonight. Meanwhile you're forbidden to leave the hotel."

We sat around in the bar for a while and when Swenson went back to the consulate I walked down to the docks to interview refugees and take pictures.

The docks and streets were crowded with people, mostly women, squatting quietly under their conical hats, feeding their children or just waiting for something, anything, to happen. But there was no panic. Swenson was annoyed when I got back to the hotel, but I had four rolls of good film so I didn't care much. When he handed out pieces of paper, which were supposed to be passes for the evacuation flight, he gave me mine along with the others, but with a stern remark that I was lucky to get one.

We took the jeeps to the airport at 7:30 p.m. and waited for the World Airlines plane in a bunker outside the main airport gate as we had been instructed. There seemed to be nobody else around except a few South Vietnamese Army helicopter pilots who begged us to try to take them and their families with us.

Then the plane landed and people emerged from everywhere, from buildings and behind bushes, and out of the sandbagged bunkers and crowded around the gate.

There was still no real panic until a us Embassy employee in civilian clothes (probably a cia man) stationed inside the gate, began to fire his pistol in the air.

Bennett, who had been sipping at a bottle of Johnny Walker in our bunker, and who gets angry easily anyway, shouted at the man to stop it. Two of us tried to talk to him but he pointed the pistol at us and then went on firing it in the air.

"You stupid bastard," Bennett was shouting. "Stop it you stupid bastard. You'll cause a panic." The man didn't stop and there was a panic, thanks partly to him.

The mass of people, perhaps a thousand of them, some waving pieces of paper the same as ours, pushed through the gate or crawled under the wires and mobbed the aircraft. us officials allowed some of them on board. I had to try to console a woman who tried over and over again to break through a cordon of armed us soldiers. Her five children had been taken on board the plane but she had not made it. Her wails were so piercing and continuous they rose above the noise of the engines of the huge jet. I talked to the soldiers and they escorted her onto the plane so she could take her children off. She was smiling when she walked away from the plane with them, back to the danger of Danang.

The plane was about half full when the pilot ordered the doors closed and the gangways removed. He taxied through the panicky mob and took off for Cam Ranh Bay. The us consul general drove us back through the eerily silent, crowded city to the Grande Hotel.

In situations like this there is a correspondents' hierarchy and it is usually the correspondent in charge of a tv crew who takes a leadership role. For some reason, if there are several network crews it is the cbs man. Bruce Dunning of cbs, a quiet ex-newspaperman based in Tokyo, called us

together in the deserted bar of the deserted hotel and announced in one of the quaint phrases that afflict TV men:
"We're going to have to activate the charter."

I'd heard about the charter. It was an old propellor-
driven C-46 which the networks and wire services had
standing by in Saigon, in a cooperative deal, in case any of
their staff found themselves in serious trouble they
couldn't get out of. It was costing a lot of money but nobody had used it through the fall of Phnom Penh and the
start of the collapse of South Vietnam.

"I can't use the charter," I said. "*The Toronto Star*
hasn't paid any of the shot. We're not in on the deal."
Again it was difficult working for an individual newspaper
with no logistical backup.

"It's OK," Dunning said. "We'll take you along as a
refugee."

To get in touch with the CBS bureau in Saigon Dunning
had to get to the US Consulate. He took the risky walk, in
the middle of the night, through the unsettled city streets,
now filled with angry, disillusioned, and disorganized soldiers, some of them robbing and looting. He was short and
tubby and was sweating when he got back, not entirely
from the heat.

"There was one emergency line still open. They let
me use it and I activated the charter," Dunning said. "One
o'clock tomorrow at the airport."

In the morning Danang, though crowded, was still reasonably quiet. The refugees and soldiers, hundreds and
thousands of them, were still packed pathetically on the
docks, bargaining in exorbitant amounts with ferrymen to
take them to the ships in the river. The normal population
of the city was 458,000. Now it was more than double that.
There was some pushing and shoving to get on the sampan
ferries, but not much. Vietnamese boy scouts politely and
effectively patrolled the docks, helping to keep order.

117

We had breakfast at the street stalls outside the hotel, dry bread and coffee which was all there was. The jeeps arrived about 11 a.m. to take us to the airport. As I checked out of the Grande Hotel, the biggest in Danang, the owner, a well-dressed woman wearing dainty brocade slippers with turned-up toes, took my money then burst into tears and began to babble hysterically in Vietnamese. A boy from a stall interpreted for me. "She wants to go with you," he said.

She took a bundle of money from the till, stuffed it in a little handbag, locked the doors of the hotel and climbed into one of the jeeps beside the eighty-year-old mother of one of the Vietnamese sound men.

The city was still quiet as we drove the first few blocks from the waterfront and then it suddenly seized up. Traffic—cars, jeeps, motorcycles, Lambretta buses, and bullock carts—clogged the narrow streets and crashed into each other at intersections. People were packed so tightly on the pavement, pushing against each other, trying to move in different directions, that it was next to impossible to move anywhere. It was hot and the sweat soaked my bush jacket.

We abandoned the jeeps but still couldn't move through the people. Fuch, the AP cameraman, with only half a face as a result of a front-line assignment a few years previously, flailed about with his cameras trying to force a passage through the mob. Y. B. Tang, the diminutive Chinese ABC cameraman and his equally tiny soundman, Dinh, were loaded down with huge amounts of heavy equipment. They used it like protective armour to charge into the crowd and clear a way for me and Dinh's mother, who seemed to be quite calm about the whole thing. Little Tang must have thought I was having trouble staying with them and maybe I was. He took my fairly heavy camera bag, adding it to the great weight he was already carrying. We left a few people spread-eagled in the gutters, but we made it to a clear space and a soldier on a Honda took me on his pillion to the airport.

There were at least 100,000 people at the airport, trying to climb over high wire fences to get to the runway. Some made it and some didn't. Their clothes were torn. Some abandoned their shoes near the fences so they could grip the wires with bare toes. A few American officials tried to keep order.

The soundman's ancient mother was there, smiling and not even sweating, and so was the hotel owner, clutching her purse full of piastres. We showed the passes Swenson had given us the previous night and the Americans allowed all of our group onto the runway.

There had been some World Airways flights to Nha Trang during the morning, but they had all been mobbed by the crowds, mostly by soldiers, so now the flights had been cancelled. An executive of the airline warned us that our plane would be mobbed too if it arrived. He went to the control tower, contacted our pilot, told him to land on a remote section of the strip, and be ready to take off immediately. We gathered our small group together, walked to the part of the strip he had indicated and waited.

But the word spread and our group somehow grew bigger, to maybe a hundred people. When the old c-46 landed, they rushed it, its motors still roaring, so that we all had to punch and elbow our way aboard. Others on the tarmac, mostly South Vietnamese soldiers and their families jumped into jeeps and on Hondas when they saw the plane land and sped toward it, surrounding it with a yelling, panicky cordon. The plane was grossly overloaded with about 150 people and we had to push others, pathetically, off the plane's ladder, sending them sprawling to the tarmac. A young woman hurled a tiny baby into my arms as the plane began to move and we were trying to pull in the ladder and close the door.

"Take him, please take him," she wailed in English. I didn't know what to do with the baby so we stopped the plane briefly and pulled the mother on board. We staggered off with our load, followed the length of the tarmac by jeeps and Hondas carrying people waving fists at us.

We thought we were the last correspondents in downtown Danang before it collapsed in complete panic and was captured, two days later, by two truckloads of guerrillas, about half of them women. We put in our stories that we were. But Brian Barron, the bbc tv correspondent, and his crew had managed somehow to penetrate the panic into the downtown area as we were leaving, to take some of the best film footage of the war and eventually escape on one of the refugee ships. The few remaining Americans in the city where the United States had first entered the fighting ten years before with a marine assault on the beaches, also escaped ignominiously by ship. The incredibly calm consul general was one of the last to leave, wading and swimming to a ship through the heavy surf, clutching General Ngoc Quang Truong, the commander of the South Vietnamese First Infantry Division, who couldn't swim.

Ed Daly, the unpopular president of World Airways, was in many ways a leading actor in this dismal drama of the last days of the American presence in Danang. He had decided, this hard-drinking, tough-talking, gun-toting millionaire, to do something personally about the problems of Vietnam. His planes and their courageous crews had been hired first for the us government's rice runs into Phnom Penh when it was beseiged by the Khmer Rouge, then for the refugee flights from Danang. They had kept Phnom Penh alive a little longer and they did manage to rescue some of the Danang refugees.

The Melbourne *Herald's* Bruce Wilson once wrote of Daly: "Mr. Ed . . . is not personable. He has a face like a red beacon fed by a hundred bulbs, thirty of which have ceased operation."

Once, at a formal dinner and press conference at the Caravelle Hotel in Saigon, Daly took a pistol from his clothing, placed it beside him at the head table and proclaimed that he would "shoot the next Goddamned man who talks while I'm talking." We stopped our chatter at the correspondents' table and walked out on him in disgust.

But Daly had his heroic side as well, and his staff loved him. The day after we activated the charter and escaped from Danang, he decided to defy the bureaucracy's order against any further flights and make just one more attempt. His chief pilot, Ken Healy, roared one of the World Airways 727s illegally off Saigon's Tan Son Nhut strip about noon on March 29. He headed for Danang, followed by a backup plane, ignoring the chances that fighters would be scrambled to knock them out of the sky. Daly himself was on board the first plane. So were a handful of journalists. Only the major American news organizations were warned of the flight so I heard nothing about it until I read Paul Vogle's story on the UPI wire, one of the most memorable stories of the Vietnam War:

Only the fastest, the strongest, and the meanest of a huge mob got a ride on the last plane from Danang that Saturday. People died trying to get aboard and others died when they fell thousands of feet into the sea. Even desperation could no longer keep their fingers welded to the undercarriage.

It was a flight into hell, and only a good, tough American pilot and a lot of prayers got us back to Tan Son Nhut air base alive—with the Boeing 727 flaps jammed and the wheels fully extended. It was a ride I'll never forget.

World Airways President Ed Daly was aboard. He was angry and tired. Daly said he had been up all night arguing with American and Vietnamese officials for permission to fly into beseiged Danang to get some more refugees out. Daly finally said to hell with paperwork, clearances, and caution and we were on our way.

It seemed peaceful enough as we landed at the airport 370 miles northeast of Saigon. Over a thousand people had been waiting around a Quonset hut several hundred yards away from where we touched down. Suddenly it was a mob in motion. They roared across the tarmac on motorbikes, jeeps, Lambretta scooters, and on legs driven by sheer desperation and panic.

Ed Daly and I stood near the bottom of the 727's tail ramp. Daly held out his arms while I shouted in Vietnamese, "One at a time, one at a time. There's room for everybody." But there wasn't room for everybody and everybody knew damn well there wasn't. Daly and I were knocked aside and backward.

If Ed Daly thought he'd get some women and children out of Danang he was wrong. The plane was jammed in an instant with troops of the First Division's meanest unit, the Hac Bao *(Black Panthers). They literally ripped the clothes right off Daly along with some of his skin. I saw one of them kick an old woman in the face to get aboard.*

In the movies somebody would have shot the bastard and helped the old lady on the plane. This was no movie. The bastard flew and the old lady was tumbling down the tarmac, her fingers clawing toward a plane that was already rolling.

122

Flight from Danang

A British cameraman who flew up with us made the mistake of getting off the plane when we landed, to shoot the loading. He could not get back aboard in the pandemonium. In the very best tradition of the business he threw his camera with its precious film into the closing door and stood there and watched the plane take off . . .

As we started rolling, insanity gripped those who had missed the last chance. Government troops opened fire on us. Somebody lobbed a hand grenade toward the wing. The explosion jammed the flaps full open and the undercarriage at full extension.

Communist rockets began exploding at a distance. Our pilot, Ken Healy, fifty-two, of Oakland, California, slammed the throttles open and lurched into the air from the taxiway. There was no way we could have survived the gunfire and gotten onto the main runway.

A backup 727 had flown behind us but had been ordered not to land when the panic broke out. Its pilot radioed that he could see the legs of people hanging down from the undercarriage of our plane. UPI photographer Lien Huong, who was in the cockpit of that backup plane, saw at least one person lose his grip on life and plummet into the South China Sea below.

There were 268 or more people jammed into the cabin of the little 727 limping down the coast, only two women and one baby among them. The rest were soldiers, toughest of the tough, meanest of the mean. They proved it today. They were out. They said nothing. They didn't talk to each other or us. They looked at the floor.

I saw one of them had a clip of ammunition and asked him to give it to me. He handed it over. As I walked up the aisle with the clip, other soldiers started loading my arms with clips of ammunition, pistols, hand grenades.

They didn't need them anymore. In the cockpit we wrapped the weapons and ammo in electrical tape.

There was no more fight left in the Black Panthers this day. They had gone from humans to animals and now they were vegetables.

We flew down the coast, the backup plane behind us all the way. Healy circled Phan Rang air base, 165 miles northeast of Saigon, hoping to put down for an emergency landing. On the backup plane Lien Huong served as interpreter, radioing Phan Rang control tower that the Boeing had to land there in an emergency. The reply came back that there was no fire fighting equipment at Phan Rang so Healy aimed the plane for Tan Son Nhut.

I heard Healy on the radio, telling Tan Son Nhut, "I've got control problems." The backup plane was shepherding us in.

Huong, in the cockpit of the backup plane, told me later when we touched down safely, the pilot and cabin crew on his plane pulled off their headphones, some of them crossed themselves and all thanked God for a small miracle delivered this Easter weekend.

When we landed the troops who had stormed us were offloaded and put under arrest. They deserved it. A mangled body of one soldier, M16 rifle still strapped to his shoulder, was retrieved from the undercarriage. He got his ride to Saigon, but being dead in Saigon is just the same as being dead in Danang.

Over a score of others came out of the baggage compartment, cold but alive. Somebody told me that four others crawled out of the wheel wells alive. One died.

The last plane from Danang was one hell of a ride. For me. For Ed Daly. For Ken Healy. For the Black Panthers. And for two women and a baby. But the face that remains is that of the old woman lying flat on the tarmac seeing hope, seeing life itself, just off the end of her finger-tips and rolling the other way.

Tom Aspin, of Viznews, who threw his camera and film onto the plane as he was being left behind in Danang, eventually climbed into the deserted control tower, pressed every button on every instrument and shouted: "Help, I'm all by myself in Danang." Somewhere he had pushed the right button. An Air America helicopter landed and carried him to safety.

The CBS bureau held his film for him. There was only a few hundred feet of it. It wasn't much good and it didn't make the air.

VIII

The End of Saigon

MOST OF THE WESTERN CORRESPONDENTS in Southeast Asia in 1975 saw the fall of two regimes. The Lon Nol government in Cambodia had lost most of its American support in 1973 and its capital city, Phnom Penh, fell to the Communist Khmer Rouge forces on April 17, 1975.

Three weeks earlier, in South Vietnam, Hue had fallen to the North Vietnamese troops as they advanced southward toward the capital. We had all known since the beginning of April that Saigon was about to fall and the war would be over. Soon after Danang collapsed on March 29, the sprawling, overpopulated city of Saigon, untouched by enemy fire since the Tet offensive of 1968, was surrounded by ten Communist divisions with six more stationed behind them, ready to plug any gaps in the offensive. The Communists' crack troops formed a circle around Saigon, nowhere more than thirty-five miles away.

The people of Saigon knew, too, and they were scared. I walked into the South Vietnam government tourist bureau on Tu Do Street one afternoon on the off chance that there might be some crazy tourists around who would make a light story, but, of course, there weren't. The building was deserted and the girl behind the counter was doing business in reverse.

"Please take me with you to Canada," she pleaded. "I am very much afraid. My family is from the north and we are all going to be killed. You must be able to arrange to get us out somehow." She was crying, her hands were shaking and she was indeed very much afraid.

The fear was quiet, unpanicked, but it was deep and everywhere. Some committed suicide. Ian Wilson, the CBC cameraman who occupied a corner suite at the Caravelle, was woken one morning by the commotion of a suicide in the square below. He jumped from bed, grabbed his camera, flung open the windows, climbed to the ledge and began shooting. He wondered for a while why the crowd below, especially the women, concentrated their attention on him instead of the suicide scene. Then he realized he was wearing only his camera.

Walking the streets was not pleasant during the last weeks. The beggars were more aggressive, the girls more desperate, and the pickpockets operated almost openly. One day one of them, a girl, approached me as I walked along Tu Do to file a story and announced frankly after she bumped into me, "Excuse me, sir, but I'm a pickpocket." I patted all of my pockets to see what was gone, but they were still buttoned down so I let her go. She had taken my reading glasses from the unbuttoned pocket on the bush jacket sleeve.

There may be nothing more pathetic than a professional observer without his glasses, even if they are only reading glasses required for looking at military analyses, maps, wire service copy, and typewriter keys. All of the dozen or so optometrists' shops in the central part of the city were shuttered, their owners safely overseas by now. Panic strikes different people in different ways and for me the panic set in when I began to believe I couldn't cover the war any more.

In desperation I asked a cyclo driver in front of the Caravelle, an entrepreneur who could get anybody anything, where I could get some new glasses. He shouted something in Vietnamese and we were suddenly surrounded by people trying to sell us glasses. They produced glasses from everywhere, from their pockets and hats and from beneath the cushions of their cyclos and taxis: horn rims, metal rims, and bifocals. Ti Ti, the jasmine girl, had about eight pairs which she produced from somewhere in her raggedy clothing. She started her sales pitch by calling me "gentleman" and ended with her usual, "You number ten cheap Charlie."

There was obviously a glut of glasses in the city and I felt better. In the circumstances I even became fussy. I told the cyclo driver I wanted a pair properly made for me by an optometrist. He shook his head at this madness but waved away the now-angry horde of spectacle sellers and pedalled me to the central market.

He found an old man in the market who sat me on a stool in a gutter and sent an assistant across the alley to hold a card with letters on it. Then he fitted an array of lenses into metal frames over my eyes until I found I could read the card clearly, and he made me a pair of glasses that lasted for years. They cost the equivalent of $7.50, including the cyclo's exorbitant commission, and I felt the sort of relief that comes after safely crossing a minefield.

The Americans and other foreigners were pouring out of the city in these last weeks on commercial airlines or the American evacuation flights, making it lonely. The Canadian chargé d'affaires, Ernest Hébert, ordered all Canadians out on two final c-130s, but he knew the newsmen wouldn't go. Cooperatively he pulled down the flag on the Canadian Embassy a few times so the TV cameras could catch it.

Brian Ellis, the genial CBS bureau chief, later the network's foreign editor, organized an amazing evacuation of Vietnamese employees of the news services and their dependents. He smuggled at least 1,200 of them to the planes at Tan Son Nhut airport in everything from cyclos to garbage trucks, with the tacit agreement of US Ambassador Martin.

The demand for the Ellis evacuation service became so desperate he had to change hotels every night, from the Caravelle to the Continental to the Majestic, in order to escape the mobs who pounded on his doors. Some of his clients produced pistols and laid them casually on their laps as they tried to convince him of their present or previous connections with the networks.

We were all scared. The correspondent who is not scared in such circumstances is stupid. But a feeling of fatalism sets in. There is nothing at all you can do about the events around you except to follow the correspondents' edict and "take care" not to do anything rash. And this feeling of fatalism is mixed with the exhilaration of being on the big story and the joy of the company of friends who are among the best professionals in the business.

There was only one decision to make: whether to stay after the fall or get out, because it was still possible to get out almost to the end, on flights sent to evacuate the embassy staffs who were leaving in droves; the Australians, the

130

Canadians, the Taiwanese, the British, until only the French and Americans remained. I even went home to Hong Kong and back on a commercial flight on April 21 to pick up some money.

Some correspondents were ordered home by their offices, sometimes because of the danger and sometimes the expense. It was costing *The Toronto Star* over $10,000 a month in insurance premiums alone for their one man on the scene. Insurance was triple that for a TV crew. Some correspondents and crews went of their own accord. One Radio Canada crew flew in in the last days and asked my advice, as the senior Canadian correspondent in the area, about the situation. They seemed surprised that there was a real war going on a few miles away with bullets and bombs.

"It does not seem to be civilized here," the *Québecois* correspondent remarked at the end of my briefing. He and his crew stayed for about two days, interviewed the Archbishop of Saigon, and took off hurriedly for home.

Peter Hazelhurst of *The Times* and I talked over our options. We made our decisions over cups of lemon tea in a Tu Do Street restaurant a week or so before the fall. Hazelhurst is a gentle man who used to be a stunt pilot in an air circus in his native South Africa. He was spending much of his time trying to "save" the girls in the Miramar Hotel, listening to their stories for hours on end, telling them they'd be all right if only they would go home to the families they were supporting. But he was scared too, and we talked of our mutual fears over the cups of tea.

We had both asked the senior members of the Viet Cong delegation to the International Control Commission, which held press conferences regularly every Saturday at their headquarters at Tan Son Nhut, whether correspondents would be killed after "liberation," and they'd vaguely assured us they would not. But we didn't believe it. Both of us, wrongly as it turned out, predicted a bloodbath when the Communists marched into Saigon.

We decided that because we were one-man bureaus it would be professionally senseless to stay after "liberation" because there was unlikely to be any means of communication with our home countries and we would be unable to file the story of the last hours and whatever followed. Better, we decided, to go with the evacuation of the last of the Americans, providing an evacuation occurred and that the Americans would take a Brit and a Canadian with them. The evacuation would be the big story and we could file it from wherever it took us. But it was a decision based as much on personal fear as it was on professionalism.

Most of the time, though, we were too busy to contemplate our personal feelings for long. It was impossible for an individual newsman to keep up with the events, military and political, in the last few weeks. A huge c-5a transport carrying 257 orphans to America crashed soon after takeoff from Tan Son Nhut on April 4, killing 155 people. I was "up the road" at the time and I heard about it from the bbc in London on my little shortwave radio. I covered myself by cabling *The Toronto Star* office and suggesting they take the wire service stories, thus letting them know that I was at least aware of the incident.

A lone plane flown by a South Vietnamese defector swooped twice over the city on April 8, bombing the presidential palace on the second run, killing two palace guards. I ran through the pandemonium of startled troops and scurrying civilians to file the story at the Reuters office, a few hundred yards away from the palace, then prepared to hole up there, near the communications system, for the "liberation" we expected to follow. But it didn't come then. A twenty-four hour curfew was soon lifted and I walked through the empty streets back to the hotel.

The huge Bien Hua ammunition dump exploded in the early morning hours of April 15. It was about twenty-five miles away but it shook the city and tumbled me out of bed.

Refugees from the north poured by ship and barge into Vung Tau, the seaside resort south of Saigon, providing pathetic interviews when you could reach them along a road cut in several places by the Communists. One large family I interviewed had fled from Hue to Danang and then to Nha Trang before finally making it to Vung Tau in a barge. They said the mother of the family had slipped and fallen during the voyage from Nha Trang and died from her injuries and exhaustion.

The family was carrying four little bundles wrapped in green military cloth and I asked the eldest son what was in them.

"These three are rice and clothes," he said. "That one there is mother."

Xuan Loc, on Highway 1, about thirty-five miles north of Saigon fell finally on April 21 after being bravely defended by the Vietnamese Eighteenth Division. It was the last stand, and the Americans tried their final desperate trick there.

They imported a secret CBU55 bomb, never used before or since, from storage in Thailand and had a Vietnamese Air Force C-130 drop it on the little city during the last days of its defense. Its secret combination of chemicals was designed to burn oxygen at such a rate it literally sucked the air from the lungs of anyone within a quarter of a mile of where it hit. It killed about 250 North Vietnamese troops, leaving their bodies oddly intact. Reconnaissance pictures showed fixed expressions of wide-eyed horror on the faces of the dead. But it didn't stop the Communist advance.

Nguyen Van Thieu finally resigned as president on April 21 to be replaced by Vice President Tran Van Huong and then by Duong Van Minh (Big Minh), but that didn't stop the advance either.

Thieu's wife, already rich from corruption and owner of a villa in Switzerland, tried to send sixteen tons of the country's gold on a chartered Swiss airline, but the pilots, for safety reasons, demanded to know the contents of the boxes. They conferred with the Swiss Consulate, then refused to fly out the fortune.

Instead, then, she had corrupt officials find her a ship which took the gold and piles of diamonds and jade to France. She also took many antiques, mostly belonging to the government, although unknown to her many of them had been replaced with worthless replicas by corrupt museum officials.

Mrs. Thieu asked her husband's military aide, General Dang Van Quang, to look after the antiques for her. Quang was a very fat man whom we used to call "Giggles." He made most of his fortune in the heroin trade while his wife ran brothels in the Mekong Delta. Quang had the genuine antiques and the copies from the museum loaded on a ship that travelled via the US to Montreal, where he now lives. Mrs. Thieu supervised the packing personally.

Then the Thieus themselves left for Taiwan in the early morning hours of April 26, on a super secret flight by a US C-118 aircraft. They carried four suitcases stuffed with dollar bills in large denominations.

I was in the antique business myself in these last days. The day before the Thieus fled, Tony Paul insisted on buying a present for his wife for their wedding anniversary on May 2, and he asked for my help. I took him to the classiest antique store in the city, on the first floor of the building across from the Caravelle Hotel, where the best of the

Vietnamese antiques had been sold honestly, though expensively, throughout the war.

It was still stocked with beautiful Ming bowls and vases, most of them so big they couldn't be carried away, and with finely carved silverware and pieces of jade; but there were no customers anymore, just the two saleswomen who had served with silent dignity a generation of the city's richer and more discriminating locals and visitors.

Paul's eyes lit on a strange looking apparatus, a water pipe, with an elaborately carved ivory bowl and a thin bamboo stem curving about two feet above it. It was a big ugly thing but it fascinated him. He figured he would be able to get it out of the country somehow and he bought it for a hundred dollars.

I was looking at the jade pieces, mainly because they were small and smugglable, but I couldn't make up my mind so I asked the senior saleswoman to point out the most expensive piece of jade they had in the store. She looked through her catalogue and pointed to two delicate, small bowls and saucers, with lids.

"How much?" I asked.

"A million piastres," she said.

I was just not used to dealing in millions of any sort of money, even piastres which were then losing their value by about 50 per cent a day.

"I'll give you $120 for them," I said.

"OK," she said, without even a smile. And she wrapped them for me in two little boxes.

Malcolm Gray, of the Toronto *Globe and Mail*, had been ordered to leave Saigon that day. He agreed to smuggle the jade pieces out for me and deliver them to Marie in Hong Kong.

"Be very careful," I warned him. "They're worth at least a million piastres."

He treated them with great care, bribing the customs at Tan Son Nhut much more than the usual amount and hugging them on his lap all the way to Hong Kong.

When I got home myself much later I suggested to Marie that we should take the jade pieces to Mr. Wong, our jeweller, for a valuation.

Mr. Wong examined the pieces carefully. "Quite nice pieces of new jade," he said eventually. "Better than some we get in Hong Kong. Worth at least a hundred dollars, maybe even a hundred and twenty."

I walked casually into the Reuters office to file a story on the morning of April 28. Pat Massey, the wire service's chief reporter, was running to the door knocking some files to the floor in his rush.

"Do you have a car?" he yelled at me. "I need a car straight away."

"I've got a car," I said, "but what the hell is all the rush about?"

He led me into the street outside the dingy little office and held a hand to his ear. "Listen," he instructed. Very vaguely in the distance I could hear the crump, crump sounds of a rocket or artillery barrage.

"They've arrived," Massey announced. "It's over."

We climbed in the car and told the driver to go toward the direction of the sounds, but he did not want to go to the war. We had to abuse him and offer him more money. At the Newport Bridge, just three miles from the centre of Saigon, on the main highway leading to Bien Hua, South Vietnamese helicopter gunships were swooping low and firing rockets that whooshed and roared before they exploded on the banks of the narrow, dirty Dong Nai River. A

CBC TV crew, Peter Kent, Colin Hoath, Ian Wilson, and their producer George James, were standing in an open jeep near the bridge entrance shouting at me.

"Don't go," Kent was shouting. "It's rough out there."

They had been trapped on the bridge with an NBC crew and some other newsmen in crossfire between defending ARVN soldiers and a small group of Viet Cong commandos firing mortars and machine guns at them. But Ian Wilson, the tough little CBC cameraman was laughing:

Damndest thing I ever experienced. There were these heavy machine gun bursts and the bullets were whistling over our heads so we all threw ourselves flat on the deck of the bridge and began crawling beneath the bullets on our stomachs, except for Hilary Brown [the tall ABC correspondent later at the CBC], *who moved along on her hands and knees. Maybe she didn't want to get her bush jacket dirty. And everybody was shouting, "For Christ's sake get your arse down Hilary." Somehow it seemed funny, seeing Hilary, arse up in the air, and with all the shouting at her, and we all burst out laughing. It was a strange time and place to be laughing.*

Massey and I walked separately to the bridge entrance. The helicopter gunships were still bombarding the river banks making a terrible noise, and the sixty-odd Communist commandos who had slipped into the city had set fire to a fuel dump on the right bank of the river, covering everything with big belches of smoke. There was a deserted roadside stall, the Thanh Huan Café, near the bridge entrance and I sat on one of its stools and helped myself to some still-warm noodles while I watched the last real battle of the thirty-year war.

The ARVN soldiers on the bridge fought bravely, standing up at times in the hail of bullets to get back a better shot. Ambulances pulled up near my little restaurant view-

137

point to carry the wounded away. It was impossible to tell who was winning.

The car had gone when I came off the bridge and as I had deadlines in Toronto I ran about half a mile through streets and markets that seemed amazingly quiet and normal. A man on a Honda took pity on me and offered a lift on his pillion to the Reuters office. Then I slept through the rest of the start of the end. My deadlines for that day had passed anyway.

Four captured South Vietnamese Air Force A-37s dropped a dozen 500-pound bombs on the military area at Tan Son Nhut air base about six that evening. The city erupted simultaneously with small arms fire, from Communist infiltrators, South Vietnamese soldiers, police and civilians. Just about everybody, I was told, started firing guns in the streets of Saigon, especially in Lam Son Square just outside my third-storey hotel window, in order to create panic or because of it.

And everybody, with the possible exceptions of US Ambassador Martin and me, knew that finally it was indeed all over. Martin was refusing to chop down the big tree in the courtyard of the US Embassy so that helicopters could land for an evacuation everybody else knew was now urgent.

Others told me the story of the eruption in the city. Tony Paul was having a drink on the patio of the Continental Palace Hotel, on the other side of the square from my room, when the bombing and shooting started. Bullets whistled above his head as he scattered chairs and tables to throw himself on the floor.

Colin Hoath, the CBC correspondent, was just about to sign off his circuit to Toronto when all hell broke loose outside and he thought the old broadcasting building was under attack. He kept his circuit open for a good live story.

John Pilger, of the London *Daily Mirror*, was conduct-
ing a black-market money exchange at the Indian tailor
shop on Tu Do Street.

"You are most fortunate," the Indian told him calmly
as bullets whined around them. "Thanks to the gentlemen
who have just bombed us, the rate has risen a thousand
piastres—but only hundred dollar bills please."

But I was taking an unusual early evening nap and
none of it disturbed me. It had been a tough day; a fairly
tough month.

The big barrage hit Tan Son Nhut airport just before dawn
on April 29 and woke everybody up, even me.

The first bombs fell the evening before, and the city
erupted in gunfire. I had interrupted my nap to have dinner and attend a correspondents' meeting in the Caravelle's
rooftop bar where we were supposed to hear about plans
for our evacuation, if an evacuation was ever called.

The meeting was vague and inconclusive. The signal
would be a statement on the American FM station that the
temperature was 112 degrees and rising, followed by the
playing of "White Christmas," presumably the Bing Crosby
version. Then we were to go to Three Phan Van Dat Street,
a block east of Tu Do, near the Saigon River, and wait. But
the US Embassy was obviously still in confusion. Ambassador Martin was still refusing to cut down the damn tree
and there was no indication of when, or even if, an evacuation would occur. So I switched on the radio in my room to
listen for "White Christmas" and went back to sleep.

Everybody rushed to the roof of the Caravelle when
the barrage hit, the TV crews crushing their cameras and
equipment into the small elevators. The air base a few

miles away was aflame. Columns of black smoke rose, spread and covered it like a low cloud. The whole city rumbled with the noise. Just after dawn a twin-tailed flying boxcar, hit by a SAM missile, caught fire and slowly circled down and down like a plane in a slow motion movie.

I filed my story about 9 a.m., picking up the news at Reuters that two American marines had been killed in the continuing attack and that Ambassador Martin was on his way to the airport and was likely now, at last, to order an evacuation. I added a note stating this would probably be my last file out of Saigon. If an evacuation occurred I was going with it.

But the copy moved slowly and I stayed in the Reuters office for a while, waiting for any more news from the US Embassy, so it was about noon before I walked through empty streets back to the hotel. Almost everybody had gone. There were a few correspondents in the lobby, looking anxious, and I asked Hilary Brown what was going on.

"They've pulled the plug," she said. "Only one chance to leave—now! Aren't you going?"

I was going. I packed my bags in a bit of a hurry, left a pile of piastres for the room boys, paid my bill, and began to walk alone toward the pick-up point on Phan Van Dat Street. The jasmine girl outside the Caravelle, who might have been Ti Ti's older sister, tried to sell me a string of flowers and called me, "Cheap Charlie." Then she seemed to suddenly relent in her rudeness. "Bye bye Canada," she said quietly. "Take care."

There was absolutely nobody on Tu Do Street and nobody at the pick-up point in front of a multi-storey apartment building formerly occupied by American families. The building itself was also ominously empty. I discovered later the departure point had been changed at the last minute because the South Vietnamese Navy had placed a machine gun on the roof of the building. US Embassy officials had some doubts about whether the sailors planned to fire on Communists or on US evacuation helicopters.

I waited for about half an hour, feeling very lonely. Then a car carrying three other correspondents arrived and they bundled me in with them to drive to another assembly point—a hospital, four blocks north.

A crowd of about three hundred had gathered near this building under a faded sign: University of Maryland, Saigon Education Centre. It was hot and the inevitable street vendors were selling cold beer. Then three ancient, gray buses arrived and we surged onto them, those of us who could fit, packed together so we could hardly move, sweating, as the one I squeezed into took a circuitous two-hour route to the airport.

A plane spiraled down from the sky and crashed somewhere in the Cholon area of the city as we neared the airport. There was the sound of small-arms fire after we passed through the gates, apparently from South Vietnamese guards who refused to allow a following bus to enter. The airport was still under artillery fire and huts and vehicles were wrecked and smoldering from the earlier attacks. A 130-millimetre shell hit the tarmac a few hundred feet from the bus, with a terrifying explosion, just as we stopped at the Pentagon East, US military headquarters at Tan Son Nhut.

Peter Collins, the CBS correspondent, had his Vietnamese wife and family with him. "Oh my God," he said. "Not here, not now."

Tony Paul was on the seat behind me. He was rescuing his Vietnamese interpreter and his family. Tony carried several of the small children on his knees along with a bag in which he had carefully packed his ugly antique water pipe. As well, he was clutching a brand-new ARVN lieutenant-general's cap, its peak impressively encrusted with gold-braided laurel leaves, which he had bought the day before for a souvenir. ARVN general's caps were going quite cheaply.

Later, when an order came to dump all luggage before boarding an evacuation helicopter, Paul refused to surrender his precious water pipe and saved his general's cap by simply placing it on his head.

The heavy metal ramp of the big chopper he ran to was just being lowered as he tried to help some of his interpreter's children on board. It settled on the end of one of his shoes and missed crushing his toes by millimetres. But Paul's shoe was trapped and he couldn't move while refugees surged up the ramp past him. A French woman tried to help him drag his foot free, but it didn't work and in the end he had to abandon the shoe on the ground.

"I dropped from the chopper onto the flight deck of the *Midway* and lined up for processing by the marines," he told me later. "When it was my turn to give my name and particulars, the marine clerk looked up from his pad, taking in this large bush-jacketed man wearing a gold-braided general's cap and one shoe and holding aloft an antique ivory water pipe with its great bamboo stem waving in the air. A look of infinite disgust formed on his face.

" 'Aw, fercrissake,' the marine demanded of no one in particular. 'Who the fuck are they sending us *now*?' "

Keyes Beech, the veteran Asian correspondent for the Chicago *Daily News*, one of the best of the old hands, was in one of the other buses. He filed this report:

We heard the bad news on the driver's radio on the way out: "Security conditions are out of control at Tan Son

Nhut. Do not go to Tan Son Nhut. Repeat, do not go to Tan Son Nhut."... It was 2 p.m. when we headed back to the city. Nobody on that bus will ever forget the next few hours.

At every stop Vietnamese beat on the doors and windows pleading to be let inside. We merely looked at them .... Every time we opened the door we had to beat and kick them back.

For no reason except that we were following another bus we went to the Saigon port area, one of the toughest parts of the city, where the crowds were uglier than elsewhere ....

I got off the bus and went over to John Moore, the embassy security officer, who was sitting in one of those sedans with the flashy blinkers on the top. "Do you know why we are here and what you are going to do with us?" I asked him. Moore shrugged helplessly. "There are ships," he said, gesturing toward sandbagged Vietnamese vessels lying alongside the dock. I looked around at the gathering crowd. Small boys were snatching typewriters and bags of film. This, as the Chinese would say, looked like a bad joss. I didn't know how or whether I was going to get out of Saigon, but I damn well knew I wasn't going to stay here. I got back on the bus .... I found myself pushing a middle-aged Vietnamese woman who had been sitting beside me and had asked me to look after her because she worked for the Americans and the Viet Cong would cut her throat. That's what they all said, and maybe they are right. But she fought her way back to my side. "Why did you push me?" she asked. I had no answer.

Austin, the driver, didn't know what to do with us so we drove to the American Embassy. There the Vietnamese woman decided to get off. "I have worked for the United States Government for ten years," she said, "but you do not trust me and I do not trust you. Even if we do get to Tan Son Nhut, they wouldn't let me on a plane." She was right, of course. "I am going home to poison myself," she said. I didn't say anything because there was nothing to say.

There was only one way inside the embassy—through the crowd and over the ten-foot wall. Once we moved into that seething mass we ceased to be correspondents. We were only men fighting for our lives, scratching, clawing, pushing even closer to that wall . . . . We were like animals. Now, I thought, I know what it's like to be a Vietnamese. I am one of them. But if I could get over the wall I would be an American again.

Somebody grabbed my sleeve and wouldn't let go. I turned my head and looked into the face of a Vietnamese youth. "You adopt me and take me with you and I'll help you," he screamed. "If you don't, you don't go." I said I'd adopt him. I'd have said anything. Could this be happening to me? Suddenly my arm was free, and I edged closer to the wall. There was a pair of marines on the wall. They were trying to help us and kick the Vietnamese down. One of them looked down at me. "Help me," I pleaded. "Please help me."

That marine helped me. He reached down with his long, muscular arm and pulled me up as if I was a helpless child. I lay on a tin roof gasping for breath like a landed fish. . . . God bless the marines. I was one myself in the last of the just wars. One American offered me a cup of water and a doctor asked me if I wanted a tranquillizer. I accepted the water and declined the tranquillizer.

IX

The Last of the Bush Jackets

ON APRIL 28, THE DAY BEFORE I arrived at the Pentagon East for evacuation, Neil Davis, the blond, baby-faced Australian freelance TV cameraman, strolled down Tu Do Street with Rick Merron, the longtime AP photographer in Vietnam. They pushed their way through the girls and the money changers until they came to the little shop, on the left side of the street, halfway between the Continental and Caravelle hotels and the Saigon River. The shop sign said "Minh the Tailor."

Minh was the first tailor to design and make the correspondents' suit, with its buttoned jacket pockets and the slots in the sleeves to take pens and a notebook. He made his first bush jacket back in 1962, before anybody knew or cared much about the Vietnam War. He had a thousand imitators all over Saigon, and later all over Asia and the world, but still nobody, it was generally believed among correspondents, made a bush jacket of the quality, style and fit of a genuine Mr. Minh.

Davis had fled from Phnom Penh five days before it fell to the cruel Khmer Rouge on April 17. He was the senior correspondent in Cambodia, a longtime resident, and he knew from his experience and intuition that in the gentle land he loved there was about to be a bloodbath.

He had had to abandon, in his flight from Phnom Penh, all of his possessions, a household of furniture and valuable artifacts, his car and his clothing, so that he had only the one suit he escaped in. And now, with Saigon collapsing around him, Davis was determined to restart his wardrobe with a genuine Mr. Minh.

Merron told him he was crazy and laughed at him. It was well known that Mr. Minh took at least forty-eight hours to make a suit, and Saigon didn't have that much time left. But Davis persisted.

Minh himself had gone by then, eventually to open a tailor shop in the United States, but he had left his head tailor in charge. Davis took a long time to pick the material for a cream-coloured suit and to haggle with the head tailor over the price of it until they eventually agreed on the equivalent of five dollars.

Merron thought the whole thing was hilarious.

"I can't believe it," he told Davis. "You're into an *On The Beach* mentality. You're nuts. You'll never pick up your suit."

And next day when Merron, one of the best and bravest of the war photographers, saw Davis standing in a Saigon street as the evacuation bus carried him, me and other correspondents to what we hoped was safety, he still couldn't contain his mirth.

"Davis can't come with us," Merron told everybody within hearing. "He's got to stay and pick up his suit from Mr. Minh's."

Davis was one of about thirty correspondents who stayed behind in Saigon, some by accident but most, bravely, on purpose. Most of them were French, British, or Japanese, but there were also a few Americans—running the biggest risks of all—including almost the entire staffs of the two major wire services, AP and UPI.

Neil Davis told me his story of the fall of Saigon five years later when he was based in Bangkok working for NBC.

Early on the morning of April 30 he went to the American Embassy. Somewhere between ten and twenty thousand Vietnamese—and a few foreigners—were besieging the place. It was about 7:30 a.m. and at a few minutes to eight the last US Marine Corps helicopter landed on the roof of the embassy. Somehow the mob on the ground sensed that it was the last, and with a violent rush it forced the embassy gates open. Soon it had the doors open as well.

The mood of the crowd was not hostile, although some were shouting Vietnamese obscenities to the American marines on the roof, who were throwing tear gas canisters down among them. Davis was swearing at the marines too, in Vietnamese. *"Do-mai,"* he was shouting, which means "mother fucker."

But there was no real belligerence on the ground, more a spirit of camaraderie. People seemed to think it was a good lark and looting had never seemed such fun. Davis didn't see one argument about who flogged what. He was offered a good-looking shirt from some American's abandoned suitcase. It fitted him too. The marines had thrown several tear gas canisters down inside the building but it barely hindered the looting. People took the strangest things. Of course the air conditioners went and the telephones, some of them still ringing as they were torn from their connections. Everything went: light fittings, desks, fil-

147

ing cabinets—the files were scattered all over the place—carpeting, chairs, anything that could possibly be moved. One ARVN soldier took the end of one of the fire hoses and marched solemnly down a passage with it. Davis didn't wait to see what happened when he finally unwound the hose to its full length and found the other end was built into the wall.

What didn't seem to be valued by anybody, however, were firearms. There were discarded M16 rifles and all kinds of pistols everywhere, left behind by looting ARVN soldiers and the fleeing Americans, but nobody gave a damn about them.

Davis went back to his Kombi-bus and found an ARVN soldier industriously removing the battery. As gently as possible he explained that he wanted to use the bus and it would be a problem without the battery. The man was a bit reluctant until Davis pointed out lots of other vehicles abandoned nearby and suggested that maybe there were batteries and probably radios and other goodies in them. The soldier finally agreed and left the van intact. Davis set off down Thon Nhut Boulevard.

The Australian had waited eleven years for the biggest story of all—the fall of Saigon—and he wanted the most illustrative film of all. Then he realized he was sitting there looking at it—the president's palace.

He drove in the back way, which was wide open, and around to the front where the wide steps led to the main entrance hall. There was nobody there. The whole palace seemed empty. But then a young man in civilian clothes, whom Davis recognized as an office worker at the palace, ran down the steps.

"Do you want to see the president?" the man asked.

Davis just nodded and the man pointed back up the steps.

"He's on the first floor," the man said.

When Davis reached the top of the stairs he found himself face-to-face with Big Minh, who had been president then for forty-eight hours. Davis didn't recognize him for a moment. Big Minh was wearing a correspondent's suit. He was unshaven and his eyes were red from weeping. He had broadcast the surrender over the radio about an hour earlier.

Davis asked him what was happening and Minh replied simply: "The other side will be here shortly."

They talked for a few minutes and then Minh walked off down the long, wide hall, his head down. Davis took film as he went.

It was all like a dream, as if he was watching a movie plot unfold. Davis went downstairs and met old Mr. Huyen, the longtime president of the Senate and Big Minh's vice president for those final hours; a good man he'd always liked because he had opposed Thieu constitutionally. Huyen embraced Davis warmly, then got into his little car. He said he was going home to be with his family.

By now the streets outside the palace were almost deserted. The people had wisely gone indoors to wait, although they didn't know what they were waiting for. Davis didn't know either. The only thing he felt relatively certain about was that if he survived the first minutes of a meeting with the Communists, he would be alive to film and tell the story.

On the palace grounds under some trees he saw about fifty ARVN soldiers, sitting quietly in the shade. There was an eerie quiet, not only in the palace but in the city itself. He walked over and saw that the soldiers were unarmed, their weapons neatly stacked in nearby military trucks. A captain walked over and started talking casually to Davis about the weather.

Then, along the street beside the palace, Davis saw a tank approaching. Suddenly a tongue of red flame spurted from its cannon and then there was the noise of the shot.

"Jesus," Davis said to the captain, "what's that?"

"It's a Communist tank," the captain replied in what Davis described as a ridiculously casual way.

"Come on," Davis said. "Is it a *coup d'état?*" He still couldn't reconcile himself to the fact that a Viet Cong or North Vietnamese tank was in the heart of Saigon.

"It's a Communist tank," the captain repeated, casually as before.

Through a break in the trees Davis saw it wheeling around the corner into Cong Ly Street, which ran past the main wrought iron gates of the palace. He recognized it, a Russian tank—low and sleek—with the number 843 on its side and the biggest Viet Cong flag he'd ever seen, held by a soldier sitting on the front.

Davis turned to the captain who was holding out his hand.

"Goodbye and good luck," the captain said.

Davis walked onto the broad lawn and put up his sound camera. This was it, the big story. Tank 843 smashed into the gates, tearing one side off its hinges and sending up a cloud of dust. The tank backed off and came again, making no mistake the second time. They were through.

The little soldier with the big flag jumped off the tank and ran toward the palace, and another Communist trooper headed toward Davis yelling. From thirty yards away, he kept the camera rolling on the tank barrelling toward the palace, but out of his left eye he could see the soldier—looking determined and aggressive—running right up to him, pointing a rifle.

"Just live another minute," Davis said to himself, "and you're home free."

The soldier was yelling and Davis put his hands up with the fifteen-pound camera held high in his right hand, and he let go with the greeting he'd practiced in Vietnamese: "Welcome to Saigon, comrade," he said. "I've been waiting to film the liberation."

He thought that ought to hold the soldier for just a second or two and it did.

Then the soldier said, belligerently, "You're an American." It was an accusation, not a question.

"No, no," Davis said. "I'm an Australian journalist." And then it suddenly struck him that if he knew much about the war and its participants, being an Australian wouldn't exactly make the Communist soldier burst into applause.

But it steadied the soldier for those vital few seconds. He hesitated and his eyes shifted focus onto something happening behind Davis. The fifty-odd ARVN soldiers were surrendering. The Communist soldier waved the TV man away with a toss of his rifle and walked past. Davis' right arm was sore from holding the camera over his head and he let it down to his shoulder and started filming the surrender of the South Vietnamese troopers.

Then more tanks came, a whole column of them. Number 843 had outstripped them in the race for the palace, the symbol of the South Vietnamese regime, to go down forever in Vietnamese Communist history. The other tanks, about twenty of them, formed a semicircle facing the palace and groups of running infantrymen joined them.

By this time two soldiers, each carrying a Viet Cong flag, had made it to the first floor balcony and they started waving the flags furiously. Their comrades below raised rifles in the air and fired nonstop bursts and single rounds for about thirty seconds. But they'd forgotten one thing in their haste and in the sheer ecstasy of the moment. Thirty feet above the two Viet Cong flag wavers, stiff in the breeze, the South Vietnamese flag was still flying. It made one more great shot for the only correspondent to cover the very end of the war.

In the palace dozens of curious Communist troopers crowded around Big Minh, who had shown dignity and great courage during his two days in power and knew what he had to do in the end. He was treated correctly by the victors and taken away to make another broadcast.

The Communist soldiers were awe-struck as they wandered around the plush palace. They found Thieu's office and one sat down in the president's chair and put his feet up on the desk.

Davis found one shy, young trooper standing alone in the main hall. He looked a bit out of it, even homesick. He was maybe eighteen years old but looked younger and the cameraman offered his hand to him.

"Where are you from?" Davis asked the standard question.

"From Hanoi," the youngster said. That could have meant anywhere in North Vietnam.

Davis asked him his name and the young soldier hesitated many moments, obviously debating with himself whether he should reveal it. He seemed to be very shy about his name.

"My name," he said at last, "is Nguyen Van Thieu." He looked embarrassed. "It's quite a common name, you know," the young solider explained.

Neil Davis went back to Mr. Minh's tailor shop on Tu Do Street several times in the next few days but it was closed, along with most of the other business establishments, as the owners waited to see what the new regime would do to them. Then, about five days after the fall of the city, as he took an early-evening stroll, he saw that the little store was open again.

The head tailor explained that the authorities had declared that he must close Minh's shop because the owner had fled and nobody else would be allowed to operate the business.

"Yours is the only thing I have to finish," the tailor said. "There are two or three other orders but I'm sure the people have gone—and yours is the only correspondent's suit. Come back before five o'clock tomorrow, but not later than five, because they'll be along to close the shop then."

Davis went back next day at 4:45 p.m. The shop was just the same, full of its many materials and ready-made shirts Minh always had ready for instant off-the-hook sales. The tailor finished wrapping the cream-coloured suit just as the Communist K4 squad—the appropriations unit— marched to the door.

Five or six soldiers lined up outside the door in single file, rifles over their shoulders. The tailor turned out the lights and closed the door. Davis helped him pull the steel mesh grill across. Then the leader of the K4 squad put a lock on the grill and snapped it shut.

Mr. Minh's chief tailor walked off down Tu Do Street without a word, his head down.

And Davis turned up the street toward the old Continental Palace Hotel, carrying under his arm the last of the genuine bush jackets.

X

The First of the Boat People

THERE WERE HUNDREDS OF US, mostly Vietnamese who were better dressed than the average and seemed to be mainly government officials or employees of the US Embassy. We were packed into the narrow tunnels underneath the Pentagon East at Tan Son Nhut airport on April 29, 1975. The occasional noise of shells exploding outside was muffled, and cheerful marines tried to organize us into groups ready to make a run for the helicopters.

At first they warned us we would be able to take only one small bag of possessions, and later they said we could take nothing at all. The Vietnamese, carrying all they now owned in the world, searched desperately through their bags, pulling out little things that would fit in a pocket. Skinny children suddenly became fat. The walls of the tunnel were lined with thrown-away radios, clothing, food, and here and there a few framed family photographs. I held onto an airline bag, just big enough to carry my typewriter, a spare camera lens, and a bottle of whisky, and I wore the Nikon by its shoulder strap. A Marine captain inspected me and said: "You're OK. Good luck."

Every few minutes a door opened far away at the end of the tunnel. Then the roar of a chopper could be heard beyond the voices of marines shouting, "Go, go, go," and the single-file queue moved a few paces along the tunnel wall.

The door opened at fairly regular intervals, like a shutter on a camera letting in a shaft of light and after one opening I remarked, to myself I thought: "I suppose that's the light at the end of the tunnel." I didn't think it was all that funny, but the American journalists around me roared with laughter. And the little joke, recalling President Lyndon Johnson's famous phrase of optimism on Vietnam, spread among some of the Vietnamese, who began to giggle as they sat among their discarded possessions, pointing along the shaft and saying in English: "Look, the light at the end of the tunnel."

Finally they were shouting, "Go, go, go" at me and I ran through the door. Marines with submachine guns were lying prone behind sandbags and there were two Jolly Green Giants, their motors roaring and rotors turning, on some tennis courts maybe a hundred yards away. The marines, flown in for just this operation, were stiff faced, grim. They looked scared and I ran like hell for the choppers.

The choppers were spending only two or three minutes on the ground, just long enough to gorge a load of about sixty people streaming from the tunnel. The rear loading ramp of the one I ran for was moving up toward the closed position as I scrambled along it. Oddly, a young Vietnamese stood up and gave me his seat as if I was an old lady on a crowded bus. The man next to me shook hands and said he was the minister for the interior, but that was the end of the conversation as the awkward big bird roared off the ground, zig-zagging to avoid small-arms fire.

At the front of the crowded cabin, a big marine with blond, curly hair swung a huge machine gun—that looked like a Browning left over from World War II, but couldn't have been—down toward the ground, then up through the air space, occasionally stiffening and aiming as if he had seen something, but he didn't fire.

While we were still ascending, still zig-zagging, a red flare swooped from the ground, creating in me the cold fear that it was a heat-seeking SAM missile. Others saw it too and clutched their seats or their children. But it spluttered out somewhere far below. And in about twenty minutes we crossed the coastline and felt safe.

It was dusk then and there were gray silhouettes of battleships strung across the ocean and the lights of scores of Jolly Green Giants and smaller Hueys blinking in the skies. We landed on the afterdeck of the *Denver*, one of the largest ships, just as a group of sailors was pushing a Huey with Vietnamese markings over the stern. Its motor was still hot and it sizzled. It was the tenth Vietnamese chopper, the sailors told us, they had pushed overboard that day after escaping soldiers and their families had landed in them.

Other newsmen appeared on the deck: Bill Stewart of *Time* Magazine, Hugh Greenway of the Washington *Post*, Nicholas Proffitt, of *Newsweek*, and a few others. We were separated from the Vietnamese and taken to a companion-way where a cheerful young lieutenant checked our passports, registered us aboard, and took away our whisky. Like all US Navy ships, the helicopter carrier *Denver* was dry.

Sailors escorted us to a huge mess, poured us Coke in big paper cups and chatted while we joined them for our first meal since the shell-shattered dawn at the Caravelle

Hotel. It seemed to be long, long ago. But it was obvious that, as newsmen, we were to be given special treatment on the *Denver* and there was talk that we would soon be flown to the flagship, *Blue Ridge*, where the other journalists were and where, we were told, there was a special communications centre for filing our stories.

In the meantime, the cheerful young lieutenant who had checked us in told us we could send one short telegram to a relative in the United States, stating that we were safe on the *Denver*. I told him I was a Canadian and didn't have any relatives in the United States. He said: "Shit. That's tough. But that's the rule. I can't do anything about it."

I sent a wire to the *Star's* veteran correspondent in Washington, Val Sears, addressed to Valerie Sears, care of the National Press Building, asking him to tell everybody at home I was OK, and that they would be hearing from me shortly. I told the sailor checking the wires that Valerie was my cousin. Tough, masculine Val got the message and passed it on to the Toronto office.

It was only a minor frustration. Life felt good on the *Denver*, and safe. A lieutenant-commander from naval intelligence took us to a wardroom and debriefed us, eliciting everything we knew about the fall of Saigon, including troop movements in the previous weeks, which didn't seem to matter much at that stage. And the senior captain of the ship (there were two captains) made a nice little speech in the mess, welcoming aboard the distinguished members of the national press.

Twice we waited on the deck for choppers to take us to the *Blue Ridge* and our other colleagues but when a Huey finally landed, however, and the cheerful lieutenant started to bundle us aboard, the US Navy pilot said he had completely lost count of the hours he had flown since dawn and was too tired to take anybody anywhere in safety. But as a consolation the lieutenant promised he would somehow arrange to send two hundred words of news copy from each of us to the *Blue Ridge* for transmission to the United States.

By now there were about ten in our group, including a CIA man named Bert, and we were packed into a little cabin deep in the bowels of the ship, with a bunk for each of us. The typewriters clacked and the stories were sent. We let Greenway file first because he was worried that the Washington *Post* would be beaten by *The New York Times.*

I took a stroll on the deck, high up among the gun turrets, alone. The sea was still full of ships, shadowy in the distance, with only a few dim lights, and the sky was still crowded with choppers, swooping to the decks, taking off almost immediately and heading back to the coast. The night was balmy. And it was peaceful.

We were all exhausted and we slept in the air-conditioned cabin, with our clothes and typewriters at the end of our bunks. A voice on an intercom disturbed us occasionally, repeating: "All third-country nationals report immediately to the check-in station in the mess."

The message didn't worry me at all. I was surrounded by my American colleagues, some of them old friends. I had just been debriefed by American intelligence and it had never occurred to me not to tell them everything I knew. I didn't think of myself as a third-country national, whatever that meant. And I slept.

In the early hours of the morning a sailor was shaking me awake.

"Are you Cahill?" he asked. "Are you a third-country national?"

"I'm Cahill," I said sleepily. "What the hell is a third-country national?"

159

"Get your stuff together," he said. "Report to the mess."

Bert, the CIA man, climbed down from his upper bunk and confronted the sailor, who was carrying a baton.

"This guy's the same as the rest of us, sailor," he said. "He's a Canadian journalist. He's been covering the war the same as the rest of us. He's with us."

"He's got to go up to the mess deck," the sailor said. "Third-country nationals have to get off the ship."

The other journalists were awake by now.

"Don't worry, Jack," somebody said. "It will just be some administrative bullshit. If they try to kick you off, we'll stop them." I believe they tried.

Bert got dressed and came to the mess with the sailor and me. The young lieutenant, our guardian, wasn't cheerful any more. "I'm sorry," he said. "Gees, I'm sorry. The ship is going to the Philippines. And the Philippines government has said it will not accept any third-country nationals. So you're going to have to be put off the ship. Some other ship will pick you up and take you somewhere else, maybe Guam. It will be all right. Gees, I really am sorry," he said. There was no doubt he was sorry.

"Oh, for Christ's sake," I said. "The Philippines government just doesn't want the country flooded with Vietnamese refugees. They don't mean they won't let a Canadian journalist pass through. I'm a Canadian citizen. I've got my passport. I can go to the Philippines as a goddamn tourist without even a visa."

"It's the captain's orders," the lieutenant said.

"We want to see the captain," Bert the CIA man insisted, and eventually the junior of the captains came.

"I'm sorry," he said. "It's an order from Washington."

"But you're over-interpreting the bloody order," I said. "In these circumstances a third-country national means a

Vietnamese refugee. I work with words, captain. I know what words mean. You can't always interpret them exactly. Have you checked with the other ships to see if they're kicking journalists off?"

"We've checked," he assured me. "Our senior captain says you're a third-country national and you've got to go."

"These bastards are crazy," Bert said. "The captain's gone round the bend. I'll see what I can do." He went away.

I was so tired I didn't care much any more.

The American sailors packed maybe two hundred of us onto the landing barge in the bowels of the uss *Denver* and then flooded the hold slowly until we floated. Then the doors at the stern of the ship opened with a roar and a hiss, and we were suddenly out in the open sea. The doors of the big, safe ship closed again and it floated away like a great swimming, gray elephant that had just had a difficult bowel movement, but had finally cleansed itself of us non-Americans.

Except for me and a tall youngish man with fair skin and snow-white hair, there seemed to be only Vietnamese on the barge and most of them looked dazed and bewildered. They had thought they had made it to safety at last on the *Denver*, as I had, and they were probably not even aware of the captain's interpretation of the order that no "third-country nationals" were to be taken on navy ships to the Philippines.

The sea was rough and the barge pitched and rolled, throwing people about. Some mothers tried to feed their children with a ration of rice the navy had given them, but it didn't work. Many of the children were seasick. Several spat out the food and cried. Some just stared at the lights from the Jolly Green Giants, still flickering in the dark sky, as they carried the last of the refugees from Saigon to big ships that we hoped would be more hospitable than the *Denver*.

The man with the white hair waved and began to move toward me, clutching the gunwale for support, and I moved toward him, trying not to slip on spilled rice or vomit or tread on children curled on the deck around the feet of their parents.

"I'm Mike Sullivan of the BBC," he said when we managed to get close enough to talk. "You a journalist?"

"Jack Cahill, *Toronto Star*," I said. We tried to shake hands but couldn't touch in the crush. "Nice to meet another third-country national."

"Crazy chaps, those Americans," Sullivan said.

We could see a few small lights at sea level in the distance and the sailor in charge of the barge steered us toward them through the big sloppy waves until the gray shape of a small ship became suddenly clear in the darkness. I had seen her before—the USS *Sgt. Andrew Miller*, veteran of the exodus from Danang, in which forty-three of its ten thousand refugee passengers died in two days. She was about seven thousand tons, manned by a civilian crew and a company of US Marines.

We had to jump from the barge to a pontoon and then climb a ladder to get aboard the *Sgt. Miller*. The women and children all made it with the help of the men, who then went back to the barge for the pathetic little packages that were their only possessions.

Sullivan's white hair must have been like a beacon to the tough sailors watching the scramble aboard and a few of them approached us as we stood on the deck wondering where to go and what to do next.

162

"Hell," one of them said, "what are you guys doing on a ship like this? We've got no water. We've got no food. We've got no shithouses. All we've got is bloody people." He pointed at the mass of Vietnamese around us and indicated that he regarded us as different. Then he added: "This is a cargo ship, you know. We're not set up for people of any sort. But good luck. Now move on."

A notice near the top of the gangway said in Vietnamese and English: "Don't spit on the deck. Don't urinate on the deck. Don't defecate on the deck. Keep calm."

A marine with an automatic rifle hustled Sullivan and me, with a group of other refugees, to the bow of the ship and we sat on the steel deck, tired and quiet, and we slept a little until it began to rain heavily. There were about two thousand refugees on the ship then and we thought it was packed tight, but somehow they crammed in at least another five thousand in the next twenty-four hours.

We were soaked by the rain so we climbed down into a hold. It was packed with people and the family we lay among had a crippled child who was also retarded, and he made sleep difficult. So we climbed down even farther into the lowest hold in the ship and found some fairly dry space among some Vietnamese helicopter pilots who had flown their families in the choppers to the US fleet as Saigon fell.

The hold stank. Kids were crapping in one corner. The chopper pilots made room on the deck among their families and loaned us their army bags for pillows and plastic bags to spread on the wet rusty metal and we had our first sleep since the rocket attack on Saigon more than twenty-four hours before.

Saigon fell at noon that day and all day long barges, sampans, fishing boats and fair-sized ships packed with people hovered around the *Sgt. Miller*, but the marines kept most of them away by firing into the water nearby.

Still the ship, apparently under orders from Washington to pick up as many refugees as possible, moved closer to the coast near the refugee centre of Vung Tau, until it was well within Vietnamese territorial waters and the coast was clearly visible.

At about 1:00 p.m., deep down in the ship, we heard booming noises and a marine shouted: "We're under fire." We climbed up the ladders to the deck and there were shells exploding in the water a few hundred yards from the stern. We could see the flashes from the shore batteries and the splashes near the ship, but we must have been just out of range because they always fell about the same distance behind as we moved out to sea.

As soon as the firing began a destroyer and a helicopter carrier escorting us sped off to sea as if officialdom wanted to have nothing at all to do with whatever we were doing.

We moved slowly, loading people onto the ship from big barges with high wire fences on the sides like floating tennis courts. The skippers of some big boats that managed to get alongside jumped aboard with their passengers and let the craft, that must have represented their life's work, drift away. There was a dog on one of them, howling.

At about 3:00 p.m. the marines had to open fire to scare away a fleet of more than fifty boats, but one man jumped overboard from his small craft, swam for us and made it. An old woman slipped and fell between a boat and the loading barge. A sailor jumped into the crunch between the two vessels to try to save her, but she was squashed into a red pulp. They took the mess out to sea in a tug and dumped it overboard.

Just after four o'clock, a South Vietnamese helicopter, with three men aboard and two motorcycles strapped to its seats, began to circle the ship. The men signalled fran-

164

tically for us to clear the foredeck for a landing, but it was too crowded. We couldn't move more than two feet in the crush of people.

The pilot made about five circuits of the deck and we thought he'd land and kill us, but then he decided to put down on one of the barges beside the ship. The crowd on the barge scattered as he made an almost perfect landing. But his rotor hit the top of the high wire fencing around the barge and broke into small pieces like shrapnel which peppered the decks of the *Sgt. Miller*. A few refugees were slightly injured.

Then angry marines pulled the three men, apparently not seriously injured, from the chopper and turned hoses on it. The motor was roaring and sparking as it tried to drive the broken rotor through the wires of the barge. The marines turned their guns on the pilot and forced him back into the cockpit to turn it off. Then they pushed the helicopter into the sea. Within ten minutes we were loading refugees again.

By nightfall we had taken on about four thousand more refugees and the work continued throughout the night. On the foredeck we were given one paper cup of water during the day, and at night a small meal of shredded fish and rice.

Our main trouble was that we hadn't planned to be refugees in the first place. The other refugees, or at least most of them, were somewhat prepared with awnings, a few hammocks, groundsheets, water containers, and even toothpaste and soap. Some of them had been on the road down from Hue and Danang for more than a month and knew and cherished the necessities of survival. But we had only the bush jacket suits we had been wearing for two days. Sullivan and I struggled for space near the bow of the ship, leaning on the gunwale and talked of our troubles.

"What do you think our main problem is?" I asked in an attempt to get down to basics.

"My main problem is I'm split up from my crew," he replied. "I lost them in the scramble at Tan Son Nhut. They must have got on another chopper and gone to another ship and by now they're probably having tea in the officers' wardroom. But the idiots back at the BBC will never understand."

There is something very pathetic about a TV reporter who has lost his camera crew and for a while I thought Sullivan was going to weep. But he was, in fact, a very tough, able, and practical man. That was the closest he went to losing his cool and his middle-class British stiff upper lip in the hard days and nights of what became a long voyage.

"You could do radio when you get back," I said in an attempt at consolation. "We'll probably both have a good story if we survive this thing."

"Radio, shit," he said. "You've got to do it on TV and you can't do that without a crew. In the meantime let's try to make sure we survive so that the bastards back at the BBC will at least get a chance to abuse me."

I began to like Sullivan and our friendship deepened as the voyage continued and got tougher. For a while we discussed what talents we had that might help us keep alive on an open deck, in the tropical sun, with apparently no food or water, but most of them were similar journalistic talents: abilities to talk to anybody, to remember facts, to make friends and contacts, to judge situations quickly, to keep calm and detached, none of which seemed to help much in the present circumstances. So we began to explore each other's private lives and hobbies.

"For a hobby I make model Tiger Moths," Sullivan said. "Not just any sort of model airplane, only Tiger

Moths. I'm a specialist."

"Christ," I said. And we both laughed. But we agreed that it might help if we had to glue pieces of wood together for a raft, or something, if we had any glue.

In fact, in the long nights that followed, it helped considerably. As a kid at the end of the Second World War, I had flown Tiger Moths briefly. So later when we were hungry we always got to talking about Tiger Moths, how they flew and what they could do. We argued about their stalling speed and their reaction to various acrobatics. Tiger Moths cemented our friendship and kept us sane.

"My hobby is sailing," I told him. "I know a bit about boats. I've got my own sloop back in Hong Kong. I go sailing to get away from it all. I'm fond of the sea. Or at least, I was."

We both laughed again, but we agreed that we might be able to make use of my small knowledge of navigation if there was a mutiny on the *Sgt. Miller* and that my ability with knots and splices, and experiences with winds and weather, could come in handy.

As we talked, other "round-eyes" appeared from among the thousands of Vietnamese on the decks and began to gather around us. A totally exhausted Spanish TV crew, who had also been on the *Denver*, came first, clutching a camera for which they had no film.

Then, through the night came:

Renée Schiller, a nice, crazy, emotional, middle-aged Frenchwoman who lived in London and had gone to Vietnam the week before it fell to pick up an orphan for adoption. She was holding the hand of a scruffy-looking, six-year-old, half-French, half-Vietnamese boy when she approached us. He spoke only Vietnamese and she called him simply "the kid." So did we. He was a good boy and eventually he learned to call us "uncle."

Anne-Marie Disloquez, a French-Vietnamese girl of about twenty-four had a wonderful smile, no bra, and big breasts almost bursting through the man's shirt she was wearing. She would never tell us about her background or what she did for a living in Saigon, but it was fairly obvious. "I like helping people, making people happy," she used to say when we asked her what she had been doing in Saigon and why she was leaving her homeland.

Mike Van Zyl, a tough South African engineer, who had lost even his passport in the mess of the evacuation was wearing the same shirt and trousers—now split embarrassingly up the back from crotch to waist—that he was wearing when he started running from the central coast city of Nha Trang two weeks before.

Akira Hayashi, first secretary in the Japanese Embassy in Saigon, was probably the most unwilling refugee on the ship. He had been on normal diplomatic business at the US Embassy in Saigon when it was surrounded by mobs of rioting Vietnamese. The Americans had pushed him protesting into a helicopter and sent him out, still in his neat diplomatic suit and tie. Then they kicked him off the *Denver* because he didn't have a passport and he ended up on the *Sgt. Miller* with his diplomatic briefcase, along with the Vietnamese refugees. He was calm, but a little confused.

There was also a very loud-mouthed American who never told us his name, but had been in Vietnam buying scrap metal. He had a habit of shouting such things as "Women and children first," and "If you ARVN had fought better we wouldn't be here." Nobody knew why he was really there, and he was no help to us at all. After a few days, he vanished from our group to survive alone somewhere near the stern of the ship.

As the dawn rose, Sullivan and I called a meeting of this bedraggled (except for the still-elegant Japanese diplo-

mat) group and we proposed that we should form ourselves into a "round-eye family." The Vietnamese, we
pointed out, were surviving as family units, protecting the
positions they had staked out on the deck and sharing
whatever they had, including moral and practical support.

Sullivan and I became the grandfather and father. We
never could work out who was which, although in the end
I seemed to be mostly trying to proclaim grandfatherly philosophies and calming people while Sullivan was thrust
into the more practical, fatherly role which he handled
with British aplomb. The two women, collectively, made a
long-suffering, frequently courageous, often emotional, but
nice mother. The Spaniards slept a lot and did little of a
practical nature. Van Zyl seemed to fit easily into the role
of eldest son, sometimes unruly and critical, but often of
great assistance. The diplomat turned out to be like a visiting uncle, who felt somewhat out of place among such a
strange family, and detached from it, although he was willing to give occasional advice.

Our first decision as a "family" was to claim a position
which we would defend as our "home," and we chose one
on the foredeck, mainly because it was the only space
available. It was a coiled piece of thick Manila rope—the
forward mooring line—which stretched beside the gunwale
for about ten feet and into the deck for about five feet. It
was unlevel and uncomfortable, and as the sailor expert of
the family I advised that we'd be the first washed off the
deck if a storm blew up, but it was the best we could do.

The sea was now glassy calm. Flying fish skimmed the
smooth surface. Water snakes slid eerily beneath it. The
sun hit down from above and reflected up again from the
steel deck so that it would have been impossible to survive
for more than a few hours without cover. We were thirsty.

The ship was still picking up refugees from the hundreds of sampans surrounding it, but now we had caught up with the main American fleet of about thirty ships, half of them battleships, half refugee carriers and supply ships. We were the last US ship out of Vietnamese waters.

As a "family" we decided that our most immediate need was for some form of cover, not only to protect us from the dehydrating sun, but so we could establish an area that would be our home and which we would defend against the crush that was growing continually worse. It was more important for us to have cover than anyone else. Our skins were fair and we were not accustomed, as many of the Vietnamese were, to long days in the open fields. The bald spot at the back of my head was already burnt by the morning sun and there was not even a handkerchief among us big enough to cover it.

We felt different and probably superior to the other refugees at this time and deserving of some special treatment. So the group decided that Sullivan and I should use our journalistic talents to talk our way into the officers' quarters and ask for blankets, sheets and string to make an awning. But when we got near the crews' quarters two big marines stationed on the bridge pointed automatic rifles at us and yelled nervously, "Get back, get back." So we got back.

Anne-Marie suggested she might have some talents more useful than ours. She combed her long black hair, brushed as much mud as possible off her tight blue jeans and undid the top button of her shirt. "*Viens,*" she told Renée Schiller in her Vietnamese French. And the two women struggled and pushed their way through the human mass toward the bridge.

Within an hour they were back. They had six sheets, a ball of string, pillow cases to make covers for our heads and a plastic bag of water.

170

Renée had a plate of chicken legs stolen from the officers' mess, where she had very briefly talked herself into a job in the galley.

Anne-Marie produced, like a magician, a small bottle of brandy, a pack of cigars, and a can of deodorant spray. She smiled and said nothing when we asked how she got them.

Much later I was presented with a National Newspaper Award for a story I wrote about this voyage and the citation stressed my "professionalism." But it was Anne-Marie's professionalism that saved our lives.

It was ridiculous. We spent ten minutes spraying ourselves and our filthy clothes with the deodorant. Despite fatherly warnings from Sullivan and me that it might be needed in an emergency, the Spaniards insisted on drinking the brandy, so we shared it. And we smoked the cigars. Somebody joked about going for a stroll around the deck. Another, of course, suggested we should ask the chief steward if we could change our table.

We took turns to sleep on the coil of rope, three at a time. And in the morning we built our tent from the sheets and the string.

But it was not a good day. Despite the small tent where we could get some relief for a while, the sun seemed to be worse and there was no water until noon, when a marine gave us two cups each from a plastic gasoline container. The marines also built six little platforms out of four-by-fours which they hung over the side of the ship for use as toilets, but there was a constant line-up, at least twenty yards long for each of them, and they were an aesthetic and gymnastic challenge.

For toilet paper we used thousand piastre bills which were not very efficient, but at least gave me an excuse later for one of my more exotic expense accounts: "For wiping arse on thousand piastre bills . . . ."

The worst thing that day was that both women began to have their periods and there were no sanitary napkins on board. A doctor who moved occasionally among the refugees gave them each a small piece of cotton wool but it was not enough and in the end Sullivan and I had to tear up our only sweaty singlets for them.

The ship was a stink, a crush, a rattling noise. Down the holds it was worse. The holds smelled of urine and sweat. Families were crowded so tight in them they could hardly move. It was so hot down there you could see the air. Hot, stinking air is yellow or purple. The people lay on sheets of plastic on the steel deck. Babies were crying constantly. They were given a cup of milk in the mornings and some hot water later in the day.

We were better off on deck, and our little house made of sheets stood up despite a bit of a breeze made by the ship's movement.

We were all thirsty, but for some reason we couldn't manage to eat all of the meal of rice mixed with sardines the marines dished out from garbage cans that night.

The sea remained glassy smooth and the sun seemed to hover only a few hundred feet over the little ship, concentrating all its rays in an attempt to broil alive the dirty, crowded cargo of pathetic people.

We were four days out from Saigon now, heading, we believed, for Guam, about ten days away, and it seemed obvious many wouldn't make it that far. The Vietnamese lay on the hot decks or in the even hotter holds. They were quiet now and you could hear the creaking of the ship. Even the babies were silent. There seemed to be no cries left in them any more as they curled around their exhausted mothers.

172

Eerily there was now no breeze on the deck where we were. I had told our round-eye family that part of the risk of our position on the foredeck would be offset because we would catch a cooling breeze caused by the ship's movement through the still air. But this must have been neutralized by a following wind equal to the five or six knots the ship was travelling. So we were in this strange and dangerous stillness. There was only the heat.

Sometimes the silence was shattered briefly. ARVN soldiers in their tattered uniforms fought among themselves for a scrap of food they had saved, their last cigarette, or a little more space on the deck. They had no weapons and not much energy. Either the marines moved among the brawling soldiers wielding rifle butts or older, wiser civilian refugees intervened.

In mid afternoon, Anne-Marie, who had seemed the most cheerful of our "family," climbed slowly and in complete silence from a bollard to the top of the gunwale. She seemed to have actually left the ship in a suicide attempt when the Spanish cameraman leaped from the coil of rope, grabbed her ankles and hurled her harshly back to the deck, scattering a group of slumbering refugee children and bruising her hip and thigh badly.

Anne-Marie was sobbing. "I had twenty-four beautiful dresses. I worked hard for my dresses. I had to leave them behind."

The cameraman kissed her. We told her there would be more dresses in France or Canada, or wherever. The Vietnamese families around us pretended to ignore the embarrassment of the disruption in ours. Eventually Anne-Marie smiled through her tears and the silence enveloped us again.

There was nothing to do but lie, when it was your turn,

on the coil of rope, or stand in the hot stillness staring at the slimy water snakes below or the skimming flying fish.

Some were worse off than we were. By now many of the children had diarrhoea and an infectious disease called pink eye, which fills the eyes with ugly pus. They whimpered quietly. Others were badly dehydrated. They lay still near their mothers. None of them died. Four babies were born, but none near our place on the foredeck.

Two French women, a mother and daughter, the owners of the Guillaume Tell Restaurant in Saigon where we correspondents often ate, had at first inveigled their way into the crew's quarters. Now, however, under the policy of complete equality for all refugees of all races, they had been expelled to the deck and were worse off than most because they had missed their chance to find a space and build a tent. They huddled together all day in a tiny space against a bulkhead, heads bowed under big, formerly fashionable hats.

Near us an Irish nun and a Vietnamese nun with a British passport sat stoically out in the sun under their black veils in their hot black habits, sometimes counting their beads, occasionally moving among the Vietnamese families, offering help with the children. The Irish nun was a big woman and we had no room for her on the coil of rope. We were being invaded at nights anyway, as the other refugee families tried to spread out just a foot or two and crushed us against the gunwale. Twice Renée Schiller woke up at night with a different Vietnamese man sleeping on top of her. "I assumed I was going to be raped," said Renée, "but I wasn't. The poor guys just wanted something soft to sleep on. Damned insulting. They moved away politely when I pointed out they were crushing me."

Despite this, we asked the nuns if they would like to sit occasionally under our tent and maybe sleep there for a while, but they refused. They could not go to the toilet boards hanging over the side of the ship, the Irish nun explained. Their habits were too awkward for the climb overboard and anyway she personally was not agile enough. In the circumstances they had had several "accidents" and they did not want to embarrass us.

We didn't see much of the marines except when they came to our part of the ship to bring our occasional ration of a plastic cup of water and the one meal of the day, rice mixed with a little meat or fish, distributed from plastic garbage cans. They were tough men with bulging biceps but many of them were amazingly kind and gentle with the children, and some were pleasant to us and apparently concerned. They brought us salt pills and occasionally sneaked us extra little plastic bags of water.

"It's the slave ship syndrome, man," one black marine corporal told us. "Us Americans have never got over the slave ship days." Then he laughed hilariously and offered a lifesaving handout of salt pills.

Some of the marines were not so nice. "You guys had better remember that you're all just refugees to us," one young crew-cut character lectured us for no apparent reason. "Everybody's the same on this ship. All refugees. All the same. No special privileges," he warned.

Sometimes, for some reason, the food didn't come, at least to our end of the ship, for periods exceeding twenty-six hours. There were rumblings of revolt among some of the hungry refugees and plans made to assault the galley, but always the handout of rice mixed with bully beef, or whatever, arrived just in time. Often, oddly, we round-eyes couldn't eat all of our small ration. The hunger was not too bad but the thirst was. My hand would shake like an alcoholic's as I lifted the plastic cup to my dry lips. It was warm, sometimes hot, but it was very, very good.

Now the ship smelled like a wet diaper. More kids had pus in their eyes and they were whimpering. But a rumour swept through the deck that we would be going to Subic Bay, the big us naval base in the Philippines, instead of Guam, another four or five days away. The sun on the deck and the filth in the holds would have killed many in those extra days. We round-eyes, selfishly perhaps, asked a marine to take a note to the captain, telling him who we were and our nationalities, and asking that if, in fact, we were calling at Subic Bay, we be allowed to get off. There was no reply.

Another day and then a landfall. We thought it must be the Philippines. Vietnamese asked us, but we didn't know.

"Maybe it is," I told at least a score of them who for some reason seemed to think we should know. "Maybe they'll let us all off," I said. "Maybe they'll just let the sick off and take the rest of us on to Guam. I don't know."

A woman near us, who had quietly cared for her family of four children, a grandmother and grandfather, but no husband, throughout the voyage, suddenly began to weep. "We won't make it to Guam," she said quietly in good French. "The children won't make it to Guam. How far is it to Guam?" She wasn't sobbing or wailing, just weeping, and she covered her eyes so the children and the old people wouldn't see.

Others pushed through the crush and lined the gunwales staring at the land in silence.

The ship pulled in alongside a dock at the Subic Bay naval base. But we still didn't know whether we would be allowed off or would be going on to Guam. Sullivan and I thought it was likely we would just take on food and water, then move on. After all, we had been kicked off the *Denver* because we couldn't go to the Philippines. But we didn't say anything to the others. Then marines began carrying the sick from the ship on stretchers and our black friend who laughed about slave ships told us that third-country nationals would be allowed ashore next.

There were cold Cokes on the dock. I don't like Coke. It was beautiful. An air force captain saw us and shouted to some sailors, "Hey, some vips here. Look after them." It felt better than being a refugee.

The air force captain told us the Vietnamese would also be allowed off the ship eventually, that *seebees* (civilians) had been working frantically for a week erecting tents for them and that they would be "processed," fed and rested and then later, probably, they'd go on to Guam. Nice, fresh, clean American ladies, the wives of officers and sailors, kept pushing food and cigarettes on us. A security officer, Captain Bill Darrow, produced a guitar and played flamenco for the Spanish tv crew. Then he sang "Saigon Girls" and a soft love song to Anne-Marie, who hadn't lost her talents. She subtly undid the top button of her shirt and turned her brown Vietnamese eyes on him.

It was hard to remember then that there were no Saigon girls any more and Saigon was Ho Chi Minh City; that the Hondas would be silent and Tu Do Street empty of almost everything but political idealism. Anne-Marie seemed sadly symbolic. Saigon had seduced the French and almost ruined the Americans. It is a whore of a city that will one day corrupt even the Communists. It seemed a long way away then, as the marine sang his love song to the dark-haired girl and she smiled that sly Saigon smile.

Darrow escorted our smelly, bedraggled little group in a ferry to the main part of the base where officers and their wives checked our identities with great and kindly American efficiency. They gave us soap, toothpaste, and towels for a shower in a gymnasium, and told us it was likely we would be able to go to Manila the next day. A young officer

177

and his wife took the two women to their home for the night and informed the rest of us, with many apologies, we would have to sleep just one more night on a ship. The officer drove us in a jeep to the *Denver*, moored at a dock.

The same cheerful young lieutenant who had checked us in from the Saigon choppers and then had to kick us off the ship, met us at the top of the gangway. "Jesus," he said. "I'm glad you're OK. Christ Almighty. Hey, welcome aboard. It's great to see you. I'll get you a good cabin. I'll tell the captain you're here."

I have never been angry, not even then, about the original events on the *Denver*. It was just stupidity. After all the Americans got us out of Saigon one way or another. They got me out of Danang. They would in the long run have got me out of Phnom Penh. They didn't really have to do anything at all.

But Mike Van Zyl, the tough South African with the split pants was angry. "You can tell the captain," he told the cheerful lieutenant, "to stick his battleship right up his arse."

XI

The Death Truck in Dhaka

TIME PASSED AT THE USUAL RATE. Jon Swain was named Britain's newsman of the year in 1975 for his coverage of the fall of Phnom Penh and the *Sunday Times* put him on staff. On his next major assignment he was kidnapped in Eritrea and held for three months by Tigray People's Liberation Front guerrillas. They marched him back and forth across their desolate land until they heard on the BBC that he was a journalist, and released him.

Sid Schanberg of the *New York Times* (which he left in 1985) won a Pulitzer Prize for his Cambodian coverage, and then wrote a graphic film, *The Killing Fields*. In it Swain, photographer Al Rockoff and the interpreter Dith Pran were the heroes and Schanberg himself was portrayed, fairly accurately, as an overambitious, self-centred loner, as many *New York Times* men are. Pran survived the genocide in Cambodia, eventually escaped to Thailand and

179

then to the United States where he became a *New York Times* photographer.

The "family" on the *Sgt. Miller* resumed reasonably normal lives. When Mike Sullivan, the white-haired BBC correspondent got home to England he found his wife had run off with the owner of their village bakery. He recovered from this and continued as a solid and reliable BBC television reporter without ever quite attaining media star status. He learned to fly real, instead of model, airplanes, including real Tiger Moths. The Spanish TV crew stuck together, at least for several years, and I last saw them covering the Rhodesian troubles in the late 70s. Anne-Marie, the bar girl who saved our lives on the *Sgt. Miller*, lived for about a year in France and then, amazingly, went back to Vietnam, possibly to get her dresses. And a fashionably-dressed Renée Schiller turned up in Toronto on a visit in the early 80s with a smart-looking youngster dressed in a blue British-school suit, who spoke English perfectly with a high-class accent. He was the scruffy kid from the ship and he still called me "Uncle Jack." He also spoke French and was at the top of his class in a posh private school. Akira Hayashi, the Japanese diplomat, progressed in the foreign service and became his country's consul in Beijing. And Mike Van Zyl, the South African with the split pants, continued his wanderings as an engineer in Europe and the Middle East.

I won the Canadian National Newspaper Award for a story about my escape from Vietnam. It was the story I tried hardest in my life not to get, but a citation on the award was for "initiative." Then I came in from the cold to a clean, comfortable North American city.

When a correspondent comes in from the cold like this he suffers a considerable culture shock. The people he meets in the plush homes and the wide, uncrowded streets do not seem to be quite real. To begin with they don't care. They are dancing in discos. They are watching a dreamland on television. They are complaining about the price of steak and the need for a two-car garage. They seem to think this is the way the world is and will always be.

But the correspondent's mind is still stuck uncomfortably on the real people in the real world and he has to stop making comparisons because nobody cares and he runs the risk of becoming a bore. It is odd, too, that it is not the excitement and horror of wars that remain foremost in his mind, but the masses of ordinary people struggling, often unsuccessfully, just to survive.

Mozzamal Haq is a real person who lives out there in the real world of Dhaka, Bangladesh, and on the day I met him he was driving the truck that picks up the dead bodies in the streets of his city.

This was November, 1974, just after a bad flood had wiped out the rice harvest and driven hundreds of thousands of starving people from their farms into Dhaka. A lot of them were just sitting day after day dying in the old cavernous railway station. Others huddled in circles in market places where they thought some charitable food distribution might occur, but it usually didn't. Some just walked the streets until their skinny legs gave out and they collapsed and died in front of your eyes.

All of this made Mozzamal Haq and his 2½-ton Japanese-made truck very busy, because Dhaka is a big city and people were dying in places scattered far apart but on the day I travelled in the van with him he was genial and cheerful, and in a way he was enjoying his job.

"I feel I am doing good," he said at one stage. "I can't feed them. I can't even feed myself properly. But I can help give the dead ones a decent Moslem burial.

"It is true that the children upset me," he said. "The children don't weigh anything at all. They are just bones so they are no trouble to pick up. But it is because they have seen nothing but starvation. That is what worries and upsets me."

Mozzamal worked for a Moslem charitable organization named *Anjuman Mifidual Islam* (Essential Society of Islam), and in the last two weeks he had picked up 327 people who had just dropped dead and whose bodies were unclaimed by relatives or friends.

My ride in his truck was worse than covering a war. There is sometimes reason, valour and human dignity even in wars. But this was a journey into continuing hopelessness, confusion, corruption, and frustration; past naked, dying little children with old, wrinkled skins; through streets where the dirt sidewalks were littered with horizontal human debris, men without an ounce of fat on their bodies, women with breasts like long empty sacks, lying there waiting to die; and some families, mostly big families, huddled around a tiny, single bowl of ugly, yellow rice liquid, their meal for that day or longer.

On the steps of the railway station there was a skinny little abandoned baby, wrapped in a sack, dying. When we climbed down from the van of the truck some pedicab drivers led us to the steps and lifted the top layers of sacking to show the baby's face. It was the face of a very old man and there were flies on it. But Mozzamal shook his head at the pedicab drivers and spread his arms in a gesture of frustration. The baby was still alive so it was too soon yet for the truck.

In a street near the railway station a mother was holding a dead baby in her arms and we stopped to see if we could take it from her. But the baby had just died and the mother was wailing and weeping so that Mozzamal was unable to communicate with her. He made a note of the place in a little book so that he would find it later.

About three miles from the centre of the city, in the district of Jatrabari, we picked up the body of a man, even though the man's family was still with him. He had been there for a while and the family was quite calm now. The sons explained that they could not pay the five hundred taka (sixty-two dollars) cost of a funeral so they helped bundle their father into the back of Mozzamal's truck. He was an older man, perhaps fifty, so it was not all that bad. The widow just stood in silence, with her head bowed, as we drove away.

At Tangi, on the outskirts of the city, there were two little children lying dead beside the road and a woman was burning joss sticks near their heads. It was hard to tell whether the woman was the mother or grandmother or just someone who found the children—at this time some young women in the streets of Dhaka looked very old. There seemed to be no grief left in this woman with the dead babies' bodies and the joss sticks burning. We put the babies in the back with the dead man and the woman said nothing.

On the way to the cemetery we stopped for a while at a kitchen in the working-class district of Malibagh, one of many such places set up by the Bangladesh government in an attempt to stem, at least temporarily, the tide of starvation deaths.

About five hundred men, women, and little skinny children, naked or in rags, were squatting in orderly lines in silence, waiting for the handout from government workers. They had been there for many hours and they showed no reaction at all to the presence of Mozzamal and me or the death truck.

The government workers carried bamboo poles to beat back anyone who tried to get more than the ration, which was one thin bread wafer, called a *rooti*, per adult per day and one between two children. As the workers went along the line, old bony hands and the tiny hands of children clutched pathetically; the workers hit them with the bamboo poles in an attempt at orderliness.

Then when only about half the crowd had received a ration, the *rootis* ran out. The workers threw the last few into the air and there was a wild scramble for them in the dirt and then a near-riot as the unfed jostled with those who had food. The unfed children wailed and the workers wielded their poles among the scuffling, scrambling adults and then it was all over. The people went away somewhere, some of them to die.

At the cemetery on the outskirts of the city the bodies we had collected were washed and each was wrapped in a cheap, white burial robe called a *kafan*. An *iman* (priest) read the *janaja* (last rites) and they were buried without coffins in shallow graves.

It cost the Essential Society of Islam 182 taka (about twenty-three dollars) to collect and bury each of the bodies. The *kafan* robe was the most expensive item at sixty taka ($7.50). Rosewater, camphor, soap, and incense cost twenty taka ($2.50) and the man who washed the bodies got five taka (sixty-two cents) each time. Gas and oil for Mozzamal's truck cost about fifty taka ($6.25) a body.

Mozzamal did not take his truck into the driveway of the luxurious Dhaka Intercontinental Hotel, where the westerners live, because he thought some of the guests might be offended by it. Instead he dropped me off down the road a bit.

I had a shower when I got to my room, poured a double scotch on the rocks and ordered a pepper steak and some Burgundy from room service. I was hungry but when the steak came I couldn't eat it.

When a correspondent comes home his memories are a kaleidoscope of colourful confusion, of wars and riots, hunger and horror, mixed here and there with some great acts of bravery and humanity, and even a little hope and happiness. He comes from a world in revolution, economically and politically, with refugees risking voyages in little leaky boats that make Captain Bligh's Pacific adventure look like a pleasure cruise in comparison; poor, confused people migrating in millions away from oppression and starvation to somewhere else, almost anywhere else, where life is bound, they believe, to be better than it was.

The world the journalist leaves is in a state of demographic upheaval, of rapidly increasing education and expectations, of ancient tribal loyalties and love of national traditions mixed with an urgent desire to advance into the age of comfort and computers. In the circumstances, only one thing is uppermost in a reporter's mind, trained to zoom in on the main point, to spew out the essential simplicity of the story on deadline.

The basic simplicity is a bunch of statistics: the twenty most advanced industrial nations of the world comprise 20 per cent of the world's population. They consume 80 per cent of the world's goods. Close to half of the other 3.2 billion human beings on the earth live in desperate cir-

cumstances, earning less than two hundred dollars per capita per year.

About 900 million people live on, or just over, the
fringe of starvation, in a condition, according to former
World Bank President Robert McNamara, "so limited by il-
literacy, malnutrition, disease, high infant mortality, and
low life expectancy as to deny its victims the very potential
of the genes with which they are born."

But few people in North America—or Britain, Australia
or Norway—are much interested in these statistics. These
hungry people are far away, of no immediate consequence.
The situation must be described another way. There are
only 280 million people in North America, a mere twenty-
three million in Canada. India's population is increasing by
one Australia—thirteen million—a year. The Chinese make
up a quarter of the entire population of the world and they
intend to become an industrialized nation by the end of
the century. Unless there is some sort of nuclear holocaust
or horrible plague, the population of the world will double
to eight billion before the present generation passes on.

Even the media, which publishes statistics about everything from unemployment to ball games, treats this grand-
daddy of all statistics with casual disrespect. Yet it is mainly
the media, with its recent huge technological advances,
that has advised the other people of the world of the way
life *can* be and the power they have to achieve it. The media has made the statistic come alive and made it
dangerous.

It is true that many of the 600 million people of India
are still too poor to own radios, but they gather in hordes
around the community set in their village at night to have
the news explained by the village elder. The natives of
New Guinea, who were still being enticed from the jungles
by gifts of the white man's magical mirrors or steel axes

when I first covered their primitive land in the 1950s, had transistor radios in their straw and mud houses on stilts when I returned in the seventies. The Vietnamese still tune surreptitiously to the BBC when they end their labours in the paddy fields of the New Economic Zones. A large number, if not a majority, of the people of Asia and Africa already have access to television. Because of the communications revolution, the Arabs of the deserts now know the value of oil. The skinny man working hard in the plantations of South America has heard the word about the outside world. He has used his knowledge to help create the new price of coffee.

The people who have fled in their hundreds of thousands from the continuing horror of Cambodia ever since Marie and I interviewed the first wave of them at Aranyapathet, still dropping dead by the thousands on the way to Thailand, are not stupid people despite the cruel Khmer regime's closure of schools and control of all information. Many are better educated than most in the West. Literacy rates all over Asia are high now, over 70 per cent of the population in a majority of the countries, 95 per cent in China, 56 per cent among Indonesia's huge population of 136 million, even 30 per cent in less advanced countries like Laos.

Some westerners claimed during Mrs. Gandhi's emergency in India in 1975-76 that she was right because a country of illiterates needed strong leadership. The literacy rate in India is now 36 per cent. That's 227,880,000 educated Indians.

To be among the minority of illiterates doesn't mean one is stupid. It means a man can't read or write. It has nothing to do with wisdom or experience. The illiterate can also see, listen, and understand. He can hear the radio. He can watch the TV. He can think.

The phenomenon is new. Never before has the combination of increasing education and amazing communications technology so vividly informed the sufferers of the world of the extent of their misery and of the means available, military and moral, to overcome the extreme disparities between rich and poor, comfortable and starving. The rich ignore the poor but the poor are watching the rich.

So when a correspondent comes home to the comfortable world he misses the reality of the death truck in Dhaka, the crowded masses, the kids crapping in the streets, the old, unliberated ladies up to their hips in mud behind the water buffalos, the queues of patient people outside the empty rice stores, the hordes of slum dwellers in the Djakarta River, creeping slowly and determinedly toward the riches of the city—and he remembers the words of the eighteenth century philosopher Chateaubriand:

Try to convince the poor man, once he has learned to read and ceased to believe, once he has become as well informed as yourself, try to convince him that he must submit to every form of privation while his neighbor possesses a thousand times what he needs; in the last resort you would have to kill him.

There were 2.529 billion people on the beat I covered in Asia alone. They had learned or were learning to read. Many of those who are not still brainwashed by tyrannical control of the flow of information, or dead or starving in countries controlled by the mad ideologues, are as well informed already as we are in the West.

We can try to switch them off as if their world is of no interest or consequence to us. But the switch won't work. They are still there. They won't go away.

XII

Return to Vietnam

IN THE SUMMER OF 1986, eleven years after the Communist tanks crashed through the palace gates in Saigon, I sneak back into Vietnam ostensibly as a tourist, but in reality as a correspondent covering a tour by the first fair-sized group of American veterans allowed into the country since the end of the thirty-year war. I find that a counter-revolution had begun in what is now a sad, impoverished but still beautiful land. The quiet counter-revolution is being led by several progressives in the leadership, mostly younger un-named cadres in Hanoi and Greater Saigon (now Ho Chi Minh City). This nationalist, rather than ideologically-bound group of reformers seem set to soon take the reins of power peacefully from Vietnam's octogenarian leadership in much the same way that Mikhail Gorbachev and his younger proteges took power in the Kremlin during the mid 1980s. And, in fact, they did that when they replaced the ancient troika of leaders, Party Secretary-General Truong Chinh, seventy-nine, Prime Minister Pham Van Dong, eighty-six, and Politburo member Le Duc Tho,

189

seventy-six, at the Communist Party's Sixth National Congress in December, 1986.

What this means, in effect, is that the economic heritage left by the Americans in South Vietnam is winning over the strict socialist structure of victorious North Vietnam; that re-education in the harsh camps where the southerners were sent to hard labour for years after the war hasn't worked; that the man on Tu Do Street in Saigon, and even also now on the broad boulevards of Hanoi, still wants a Honda instead of the ubiquitous bicycle and intends to get one. Despite the efforts of the Communist conquerors, Vietnam is still two countries: the capitalist South, which is virtually a big, black market and the North, still mainly as it was envisioned by Ho Chi Minh, a mixture of socialism and dedicated nationalism.

And the South is going its own way, apparently not much daunted by the rule of northern Hanoi, which seems to have little control over events or even the economies of the country's provinces. For instance, the Vietnamese currency, the dong, which has just been controversially devalued overnight to one new dong for each ten old dong, has an official exchange rate in the capital of Hanoi of fifteen to the US dollar. But in the ancient spiritual capital of Hue, the official rate is 130 dong to the dollar, and in Saigon (which is still the name of the downtown section of Ho Chi Minh City) nobody seems to take much notice of any official rate at all, and the dollar is worth 200 to 210 dong on the black market.

There is an old saying in Vietnam, that the king's rule ends at the village gate. Now it is obvious that Hanoi's rule ends at the provincial borders. It is clear, too, that the country is diverse, both economically and ideologically, though grimly united in poverty, underdevelopment and in the sad struggle of sixty million civilized people to survive what must be the world's most pathetic human situation.

In response to this situation and the counter-revolution occurring against it, the Vietnamese government has acted drastically, even before the December congress, by moving even more towards free enterprise than neighbouring China. It has abolished the subsidized distribution of food and other essentials to employees and provides cash compensation instead; grants decision-making powers to managers of enterprises; allows an expanding private industrial sector to employ up to ten employees per business; grants provincial governments the right to engage in import-export; proposes export processing zones and a new foreign investment code which would allow 100 per cent foreign ownership with a guarantee of no nationalization; and has decided to cut the country's unweildy bureaucracy by 10 to 25 per cent. And even more important to the ordinary Vietnamese, a fairly new contract system allows them to sell on the open market any products produced from the communal paddy fields that exceed a fairly low and constant quota, as well as the produce from their own private plots. By 1986, this has already increased overall productivity of rice by between 15 and 20 per cent to an annual production of almost nineteen million tonnes, nearly enough for self-sufficiency.

It is ideologically impossible, of course, for the party to even suggest that the country could learn from the formerly non-communist South and from observation it does not appear that the people of the South are personally any happier or healthier than those of the North, but the official press has been lauding the South's example for its "dynamism and innovativeness in business transactions." And although the United States and many other Western nations continue to treat Vietnam as a pariah country, isolating and impoverishing it since its invasion of Kampuchea in 1978, some Western countries—Belgium, Sweden, Japan, Australia, and Canada among them—are doing small amounts of business and trade, mostly in dried shrimps, condiments and tailored shirts, and some are providing development aid. But it is not enough to make much difference. Nor is the one billion dollars a year that the Soviet Union is pouring begrudgingly into a country whose people dislike Russians with an almost unanimous intensity. The Vietnamese prefer Americans, who were, after all, just another temporary enemy for a short period in a long history of many enemies and many wars. (The Vietnamese contemptuously call the dour Russians, who are essentially the only non-Vietnamese around, "Americans without money.")

But despite these small hopes for revival of a now-desperate land that was once a jewel of the Orient, there is still a long way to go to reach a standard of living for the people that could even approach an acceptable level. A decade after the end of the war Vietnam is still one of the world's poorest countries. Estimates of its per capita gross national product hover between $120 and $200, which place it alongside Bangladesh, Burma and Nepal. At last count in 1984, the International Monetary Fund estimated Hanoi's external debt at $6.7 billion, its trade deficit at $1 billion and foreign exchange reserves at only $17 million.

So the homeless still sleep on the streets of Saigon, the skinny children beg as persistently as ever and the one-legged ex-servicemen hobble along. The women work hard in the paddy fields, plodding thigh-deep in the mud behind the water buffalo or laboriously shovelling water in baskets from one paddy to another where a small simple pump would do the job. A Saigon doctor, trained in France, an intellectual man just out of re-education camp, earns 285 dong a month, the equivalent of about $1.55. He survives, like many others in the South, on the black-market sale of small radios and similar "gifts" from friends abroad.

I get into Vietnam this time using one of the oldest tricks in the correspondents' trade. Journalists are not allowed with this tourist group, or at least they are forbidden except under special circumstances and with special permission, according to the bureaucratic materials that reached me.

Let me digress here: There is not a real understanding of this journalistic problem of inaccessibility among the general public or even among some of the executives of the media. It is not realized that more than half the world is closed to the journalist these days although it is, in general, open to the businessman or even the tourist. Businessmen and tourists bring money. Journalists bring questions. Nothing in the passport arrangements between countries provides for this discrimination against journalists unless it is under a catch-22 phrase concerning the inadmissibility of undesirables. Still the foreign correspondent is regarded almost everywhere as a different breed from his fellow man and dangerous. At most of the world's airports he is now hustled aside and if he is not what the Chinese call a "friendly personage"—usually an academic with a built-in bias posing as a journalist—he is tossed in jail, tortured or worse. He is indeed an endangered species who will one day startle indifferent employers by asking for "discrimination money" in his contract because his profession cuts him off from such a huge part of the world he lives in, as if he suffers from perpetual smallpox.

There are ways, of course, to beat the bureaucracies, but they are becoming more difficult as the bureaucracies at home get bigger and more dangerous and the bureaucrats abroad become more isolationist and aware of the tricks a correspondent can play. One absolute necessity, I always found in my years abroad, was to carry a large batch of blank letterhead paper from the head office which could be filled in to fit any unpredictable complications. Very often, when a correspondent does get into a country, he is asked for something weird, like a letter from his head office personally addressed to the deputy head of the telecommunications office—whose name is unpronounceable, let alone predictable—promising that wire transmission costs will be paid in piastres or dong or baht or whatever. He may be asked to produce a declaration from his editors that he will submit his copy to a certain censor, who must be named; or for a letter of introduction to the president of the country, who might have been an unknown sergeant before the coup of the previous week; or a guarantee from the head office that it will take full responsibility if the correspondent gets drunk or molests any of the local women.

No real problem. The experienced correspondent always has just such a properly-worded letter back in his hotel room which he'll produce next time he comes to the ministry of information. For the sake of consistency I always used the forged signature of Mark Harrison, partly because his title of executive editor of *The Toronto Star* seemed to impress bureaucrats (although it was in fact meaningless in the *Star* executive hierarchy) and partly because Mark was a former foreign correspondent who would understand. (He's now the editor of the Montreal *Gazette*.) My wife, Marie, would pre-sign blank letterheads she put in my baggage with Mark's signature, and he became an authorizer and introducer all over Asia for activities and entrees he wouldn't care to contemplate.

Sometimes, though, a blank, pristine letterhead was

better than a genuine, Marie-signed Mark Harrison. Several times in Vietnam in the 70s and once in India—when lowly bureaucrats blocked my journalistic way because I did not have the ever-necessary letter of introduction—I produced a blank letterhead and wrote, in front of the bureaucrat, in big print: "This is a letter of introduction," and I signed it myself. They let me pass.

But it isn't all that much of a challenge this time to get back into Vietnam as a tourist. I give my occupation on the official forms as "author" and make my literary agent, Beverley Slopen, my employer. All that seems to matter was that I'm not a journalist for *The Toronto Star*, and it works. Oddly, though, on the way in to Bangkok I find that, without any bureaucratic explanation, there are two properly-accredited American journalists on the tour, providing they act only as tourists: Terry McDermott, of the *Seattle Times* and photographer Bob Ringham, of the *Chicago Sun-Times*, both of them veterans of the war.

We are an odd group of sixteen. Seven, including McDermott and Ringham, are Vietnam veterans. There had been a suspicion among some at my Canadian newspaper, including myself, that veterans anxious to go back to Vietnam would likely be Rambos, but this is not so. The American vets are sensitive, intelligent, thoughtful, articulate, mostly mildly-successful, middle-class men in their mid-thirties, and most of them had been badly wounded in Nam although it isn't obvious any more. Embarrassingly, the only Rambo-type in the group is a Canadian who had not fought in the war at all. The Americans are going back to find themselves, to discover what the war they had fought when they were eighteen years old was all about and to purge themselves of something, although they aren't quite sure what it is. Several of them tell me after long interviews with them that I am the first person to really talk to them about their feelings and experiences in the eighteen or so years since they returned home after fighting the only war America had lost since the unsuccessful invasion of Canada in 1812. Even their mothers and fathers have refused to discuss the war with them, they say, and when they walk into bars where old friends meet they are shunned. So they are going back to find themselves, to end all of that loneliness, frustration and stupidity they are suffering for what they thought as youths was a noble and patriotic act. They are tough men, but they are nervous about going back.

The Rambo-Canadian, named Mike, from northern Ontario, says he is interested in wars as an amateur historian. He has been in the Canadian Army for a while and insists, embarrassingly, on wearing a camouflaged combat cap, of the type Americans wore in the war. When he waves to children from buses in Vietnam he sticks his arm out stiffly, as in a Nazi salute. In the end, in fact, he proclaims that he is a neo-Nazi who thinks Adolph Hitler was one of history's great men and that all Indians and people with AIDS should be exterminated. The Americans call him "The Ugly Canadian."

Among the others is Angela Giron, an American actress from Montreal, who is working on her first novel which has scenes set in Saigon—a gutsy, attractive little lady who weighs no more than ninety pounds but has no trouble at all in keeping pace with the tough ex-servicemen.

The country is diverse. So are the people on this emotional and sometimes scary return visit. So the story is best told in vignettes:

It is only a two-hour flight from bustling, car-crowded, sinful, Americanized and prosperous Bangkok to Hanoi in North Vietnam, but ideologically it is the longest journey in the world. The tread is gone from the tires of Air Vietnam's ancient Soviet T135 jet and the cord is showing through the rubber. When the air conditioning is switched on the cabin fills suddenly with smoky vapour, as if a shell has exploded.

And there is the diplomatic problem of the hats. I am assigned to try to politely persuade the other Canadian to remove his camouflaged battle cap, but he does so only for a while then puts it back on again. The Americans try to talk Big John Raths out of wearing a red cap with the badge of the US Marine Corps emblazoned on the front, but Big John is tenser than most and bigger than all. He wears the cap like a security blanket and nobody can talk him out of it.

All of the American veterans are tense, even, they told me later, afraid. They had been taught in their boot camps, they say, that the gooks were bad people who had to be killed or they would kill you; that communism was evil and its spread must be stopped; that you could not trust any Vietnamese because any of them could turn out to be the enemy. After the plane lands at Hanoi's primitive airport a small Vietnamese emerges from his seat carrying a toy rifle. It looks like an M16, and Tim Manigan, who had been badly wounded near Saigon, jumps instinctively from his seat as if to grab the little man from behind, then sits down, grinning sheepishly. At the airport terminal, while customs people examine every inch of our baggage and count every cent of our money, Big John appears to be in a state of shock. We have to yell at him to make him move. He will not talk. He just stares into space from behind his thick glasses and under his perpetual red Marine Corps cap.

"I was taught to hate these people," he tells me later. "They killed a lot of my buddies. I'm not a man who scares easily, but there at the airport I was afraid of them."

At dusk Hanoi is one of the world's most wonderful cities. It's wide boulevards are lined with flowering trees, and its old street-lamps glow romantically. The huge old mansions of the French colonialists are still magnificent. A peaceful lake shimmers in the centre of a place few westerners have seen since the start of the American involvement in the war over two decades ago. But it's hard to love Hanoi as much in the morning when the light reveals cracks in the yellow walls of the stately old homes, the green slime climbing over them, the crumbling roofs and the way people are packed into the houses—hundreds of them now, when in the colonial days there were just the master and madame and a few servants. Now Hanoi is like an old French lady who obviously was once beautiful but has run out of make-up.

There are no cars here, only the occasional truck, a few modern Japanese-made buses and a rare little Honda 50 motorcycle. The old street-cars, installed by the French in the 1930s, still rumble their crowded way through a few of the narrower back boulevards which are constantly packed with bicyclists, cyclos (pedalled taxis), old ladies under conical hats pulling heavy loads in carts and younger ones, pouncing along briskly in the heat with heavy burdens of fruits and vegetables in their shoulder baskets. This is a poor city. There is not much in the stores, and the fly-covered fresh meat in the street markets is rare and apparently too expensive for most. But it is not, on the surface at least, an unhappy city and most of the myths about it, grown in the West during the years of isolation, are wrong.

In the late 1960s and 1970s, the Americans, for instance, were supposed to have dropped on North Vietnam, an area the size of Texas, triple the bomb tonnage dropped on Europe, Asia and Africa during World War II. So the image of Hanoi and its port of Haiphong, sixty miles away, has been one of devastation and rubble. But the fact is that both large cities are intact, hardly scratched, although a single run of B52s would have toppled half of their ancient, gracious buildings. It is true that the bridges around Hanoi, the railway yards outside the city and the docks at Haiphong were hit repeatedly. There is still twisted metal to attest to that, although the bridges have now been replaced with modern, four-lane structures. But in Hanoi all the official Vietnamese can show for the bombings—including the infamous, massive, Christmas bombing of Hanoi, ordered by President Richard Nixon in 1972—is a monument in a little back street where a single house once stood. It must have been hit by a very small bomb because the old houses on either side of the hole in the ground are still standing.

When our group left bustling Bangkok for Hanoi we stocked up with Scotch, at twelve dollars a bottle at the Bangkok airport, in the belief that we wouldn't be able to buy a drink during the northern part of our two-week journey through the isolated country. At the Thang Loi Hotel, where we are staying in Hanoi, there are unlimited amounts of Scotch for sale at five dollars a bottle. The best Russian vodka is two dollars a bottle. A bottle of very good

French wine costs three dollars and a can of icy cold Heineken beer is fifty cents.

There is also a disco at the hotel on Saturday nights, with good-looking Vietnamese girls in blue jeans or trendy outfits gyrating to loud American rock music under pulsating lights. There are a few other discos in downtown Hanoi as well, mostly in other hotels, which are packed with young Vietnamese, although admittance is the equivalent of about $2.50 in a city where mid-level government workers earn twenty to thirty-three dollars a month.

Our hotel, built fairly recently by the Cubans on the banks of the Red River, a few miles from the city centre, is clean, modern, air-conditioned and comfortable. It is also full of glum Russians, who do not reply when the Americans say "hi" as they pass in the corridors. The Russians also insist on forks to eat the hotel's excellent Vietnamese meals, while the Americans stick gamely with their chopsticks, which seems to prove something or other. There aren't many women around and the Russians keep making passes at Angela, the little, aspiring novelist in our group.

On Sunday afternoon a few of us visit a floating restaurant on the lake near the centre of the city. It is blasting rock music of the sixties era. There is only crushed papaya mixed with ice to drink. But most of the young patrons are wearing blue jeans and the waitresses wear neat uniforms that look suspiciously like McDonald's. This is not typical, of course. All but a few of the people of Hanoi are so pathetically poor they cannot afford a cyclo ride to a disco. But it causes the American journalist, Terry McDermott, to mutter over and over again: "Why do we Americans have to corrupt everything. Everywhere we go we corrupt it. Hell, we haven't even been in Hanoi yet and we've corrupted the place."

Famine in Bangladesh, 1974. Millions starved. Hundreds of thousands died.

The Dhaka death truck was too early to pick up this starving baby at the Dhaka railway station in 1974. The driver promised to come back later.

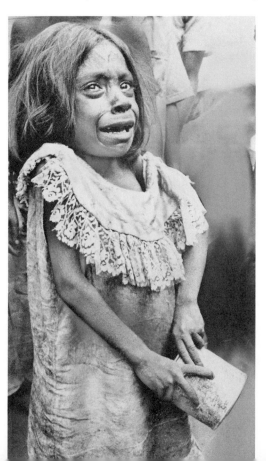

Her face is old beyond her years. The food rations ran out before she could fill her pail after lining up for hours in Dhaka during the 1974 Bangladesh famine.

Piles of wreckage of US planes are star exhibits at the War Museum in Hanoi, 1986.

A one-legged ex-soldier hobbles in the streets of Danang, once filled with US troops (1986).

Swimmers frolic now on the beach at Danang where the first US combat troops—3,500 US Marines—splashed ashore on March 8, 1965.

Saigon's Tu Do Street in 1986. Communist soldiers have replaced the girls.
Bicycles have replaced most of the Hondas.

Black-market stores thrive today in Ho Chi Minh City (formerly Saigon)
despite Communist rule. A small Sony ghetto blaster costs about $3,000 at the
official exchange rate and $225 on the black market, still very expensive for
the Vietnamese.

American veteran John Raths, 37, back in Vietnam in 1986. "When we got home they treated us like dirt."

American vet Bob Ringham, 37. "It's not like on TV. In war, people die very ugly."

American vet Mike Castellano, 37. At mass in Hanoi eleven years after the war he clutched the hand of an old Vietnamese and said, "Peace."

American vet Tim Manigan, 37. "It's not that people hated me for being there. It was more that they were embarrassed."

American vet Chuck Porzelt, 38, who skippered a patrol boat on the Mekong River during the war. "I killed some Viet Cong and this was close-up killing. You could see who you were shooting."

Angela Giron, actress and aspiring novelist, who returned to Vietnam with the American veterans.

Jack Cahill, with children in Hanoi, 1986.

Photo by Angela Giron

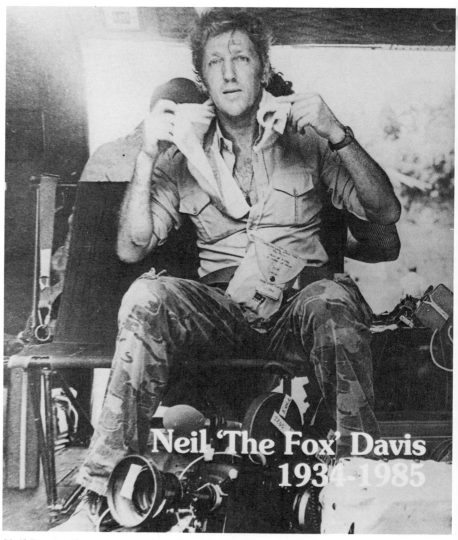

Neil Davis, the correspondents' correspondent. Picture appeared on the cover of the November, 1985 issue of the Foreign Correspondents Club of Thailand *magazine.*

Going to church in Hanoi starts out as just a journalistic stunt. During the war I had known many of the northern Catholics who had fled south in their millions in the mid-1950s, whole villages of them, to escape the communism of the north. They were attracted by the more congenial regime of Ngo Dinh Diem, whose ancestors, like their own, had been converted to Christianity centuries before. And I had briefly covered the flight of more Catholics, at the end of the war, as the South Vietnamese fought desperately at Xuan Loc, the last bastion to fall before Saigon. The Catholic Church, in fact, left a deeper imprint on Vietnam than on any other Asian country apart from the Philippines. And I had been interested in recent months in the increasing power of the Church in Poland, the Philippines and South and Central America.

So when a Vietnamese official asks if there is anything special we'd like to do, I say—simply for journalistic purposes because I have not been to mass in a long time—that I want to go to mass on Sunday. He is not much perturbed. He says he will see what he can do. And he eventually arranges to take some of us to mass by bus if we'll get ourselves ready by 6:30 in the morning.

St. Joseph's Basilica, in what is now one of the poorer parts of Hanoi, is a huge and classical cathedral, built in the French style a long time ago, but still sturdy, with stained-glass windows of enormous beauty, beggars at the portals and a packed congregation that seems to be as poor as it is ardent.

It is explained to us by the North Vietnamese official that the church has no connection with Rome any more. This is not apparent in a mass being said in Vietnamese by a middle-aged priest in red garments, under the subdued light of the stained glass, while the packed congregation— women on one side of the aisle and men on the other—

201

sing the same old hymns, but in their own language. I am so moved by all of this that I go with Angela and some of the American veterans to communion. The priest glances up briefly as he places the Host in the mouths of what must have been the first, sweaty white faces he has seen in his cathedral for many years. "Welcome," he says briefly to each of us in English.

Then at that time of the mass when members of the congregation turn toward each other and utter a word of greeting, the American vet Mike Castellano, who has talked about how the planes from his carrier in the Bay of Tonkin had bombed the hell out of North Vietnam, clutches my hand and that of an old Vietnamese man.

"Peace," Castellano says.

Oddly, in Latin, the old man replies, "Pax," which means peace.

"Peace," I say.

And the old Vietnamese man holds onto our hands for a long time, and I am glad I have come to mass.

Nationalism is still extremely strong in North Vietnam. Ho Chi Minh, the small, frail, intellectual patriot who led his people in their revolt against French colonialism and their resistance to the Americans until he died in 1969, lies in a mausoleum in the centre of Hanoi. A quiet, reverent queue files constantly past the embalmed body, which looks alive. There are many little children in the long lines waiting outside the mausoleum, as cute as can be in their Sunday best, all wearing shoes even if they are only rubber flip-flops; one wearing a Mickey Mouse T-shirt, another a Levi cap, and some of the tiny girls are made up with rouge and lipstick for the occasion.

There are, in fact, small children everywhere in North Vietnam, crowding the narrow village streets or working at a very early age in the paddies, often on the backs of water buffalo. The country's population has increased enormously from 52 million in 1976 to over 60 million in 1986; more than replacing the four million who were killed in the war (compared with 58,000 Americans) but constantly absorbing dramatic increases in rice and other food production. Most of the children look healthy enough, but Canadian Louise Buhler, from Saskatoon, says malnutrition is a serious problem in the cities while the situation is improving somewhat in the countryside. She has wandered Vietnam since 1982 organizing small (about $500,000 a year) irrigation aid projects for the Mennonites, without any government support, and probably knows more about the country than any westerner.

Now we have been in North Vietnam for about a week and Big John Raths, the ex-marine with the red Marine Corps cap, who was stricken dumb with fear on arrival at the Hanoi airport, sits on the banks of the Red River and talks. He is thirty-seven years old, a construction worker and part-owner of a bar in Munroe, Michigan, and his wit and gentleness have made him popular among his fellow vets and others in this first post-war tourist visit to Vietnam:

It was the intensity of the way they looked at me at the airport that bothered me and made me afraid [Big John says]. *We used to have POWs and they had this intensity, this hate in their eyes. And they taught us in the boot camps to hate them. And when I first got here I felt that hatred all over again.*

I mean, when you were fighting you had to hate these people. That's just the way it is. When it comes to the fighting you just don't have time to make any mental adjustments.

203

When I came out here with the Marines [in 1967] *I believed in the war. I was brought up Catholic, waving the flag, you know. I always thought that we came here for a purpose, to stop the flow of communism or socialism or whatever you want to say. When you're young you have these ideals.*

I was in combat situations for nine months, mostly around the Qua Viet River, Quang Tri, Hue and Khesanh. A lot of my buddies were killed and I killed a lot of Vietnamese. The first time I hit somebody it was a Vietnamese corpsman [medic] *who was running over to help someone else. He had no reason to get up and run like he did unless he was a medic and now I feel bad about that because he was there to help.*

Those situations are over in two or three minutes, you know. There's a barrage and gunfire and noise and confusion and people running everywhere and then its all over with and there are dead people and dead quiet and there's just this fear left in your stomach.

Well, I killed a lot of Vietnamese. Sometimes it's hard to tell how many because firefights are just this mass confusion. But it takes a lot of hatred and animosity to look down your rifle and squeeze.

We didn't lose the war in the field, you know. Sure there were sometimes we were beaten, but overall we didn't lose in the field. We lost in the streets back home.

And then when we got home they treated us like dirt. Nobody wanted to talk to us about it. Nobody said thank you. It was just like we didn't have any emotions. You know, we were only eighteen or nineteen years old and you've got to remember most people don't experience death until they are in their late twenties or thirties when their parents die or one of the family gets killed in a car wreck or something. But when we saw death as common

204

*as we did and for me to come back to the United States
and be treated like dirt by the people was pretty bad. At
least our own government or the military could have said
something to us, but they didn't say anything at all. Never
once did they ever say thank you.*

*It made no sense. We weren't youngsters any more. It
took ten years for our bodies to catch up with our minds.
But nobody said thank you. Nobody asked what unit we
fought with. When we walked into bars it was just like we
were garbage. And we weren't even old enough to drink
in the bars, for God's sake, just old enough to die.*

*Then as the years went by I began to realize that it
was the two militaries, ours and the South Vietnamese,
that wanted the war. The people in this country had
nothing to do with that decision. They didn't want us here.
The governments were doing things for their own political
reasons. And I think now that what our government did to
us should be held against them and they should be made
to account for it. The people who were responsible at that
time, who put the Vietnam veterans through what they did
and then made no effort whatsoever to show us respect
when we got home, should be held to account for it.*

*I was upset at the [Hanoi] airport, as you know, but it
was just seeing the soldiers and the uniforms that got me at
first. But now I was just talking to one Vietnamese man
who fought for nine years. He was fighting around Saigon
at the end. I mean, that's total dedication. And he shook
my hand and we talked together like old soldiers and he
said we should be friends now and I think we should be.*

*Now I think the war is over for all of us. We came into
Vietnam acting like big shots. We wanted to run the thing
like big shots and it got dumped on us. We can't hold that
against these people. Now the American government
should get off its high horse and recognize this country and*

start doing something to help these people. They've got a lot to offer us. They're the hardest working people I've ever seen.

The people of America have got to realize that what's being fed to them about Vietnam through Hollywood and TV is a bunch of crap. This business about returning the bones of American MIAS [missing in action] *is a bunch of emotional crap. Any suggestion that there are still American prisoners alive in Vietnam is even more crap. I used to be on body-bag duty. Who knows whose bones were whose and what does it matter any more?*

Americans should realize that we owe it to these people and once you get these people as a friend, as true friends, they'll be friends forever.

Anyway, I came here looking for something. I didn't know what it was when I came over here and maybe I still don't know. . . . But now I feel better. I feel straightened out right now. It's over. These are nice people.

XIII

The Ghosts of Saigon

IT'S LONELY NOW IN VIETNAM. The people are isolated and the lonely feeling clutches at the visitor as well. These people are not brainwashed as the Chinese and Soviets can be. They know what is going on in the outside world. They hear the BBC and the Voice of America and their own press is not strong enough to disillusion them. In the circumstances, their images of the capitalist West are exaggerated so that some Western countries—the United States, Britain, Australia, Canada, Norway and Sweden in particular—become much more fortunate and desirable in their minds than they really are. So Vietnamese authorities and ordinary citizens are almost desperate these days for a renewed relationship with the United States and the rest of the West; a step that might lead to economic recovery for their sadly impoverished country.

Their desperation reveals itself in the way the few Americans allowed into Vietnam since the evacuation of

Saigon in 1975 have been treated, with an importance that goes much further than the normal Vietnamese politeness. You can see it in the obvious dissatisfaction with, and dislike of—at least among the ordinary people—their Soviet benefactors. It now also shows in the sort of official attempts to attract adventurous American and Canadian tourists—especially American Vietnam veterans, for which this first tour of ours was a test—to a country that is beautiful, fascinating, but by no means ready yet for the sort of traveller who requires coddling and the comforts of home.

But the United States has been delaying recognition, and the trade and aid that would follow, until probably it will be too late. This is partly because the US has continued to recognize the genocidal regime of Pol Pot in Kampuchea since the Vietnamese invaded its neighbour in 1978. It's also because of emotional and politically delicate claims by some US citizens and groups that the Vietnamese are still holding the remains of some MIAs and even up to 450 live prisoners of war.

The live prisoners claim is ridiculous, having been dismissed by almost all of the few westerners who have been allowed into Vietnam since the war, including official congressional delegations, leaders of the American Vietnam Veterans' Association, and the veterans I am travelling with. They all admit it's possible some servicemen's bones have not been accounted for, as in all wars, but insist that the presence of any live Americans is highly improbable, unless perhaps there are one or two living willingly and happily among remote tribesmen.

The recent period of American involvement in Vietnam began in the 1940s when the American Office of Strategic Services (OSS), the wartime precursor of the Central Intelligence Agency, established a headquarters in Kunming, capital of China's Yunnan province, and had responsibility for events in Vietnam. "There, during the war," according to Stanley Karnow in his *Vietnam: A History*:

> *. . . the Allies were caught up in a jumble of intrigue, political romanticism, and oriental exoticism. Clandestine American operatives, many quarrelling among themselves, clashed with covert French agents, also locked in factional disputes. Chinese officials manipulated the Westerners and tried to advance their favorite Vietnamese while cashing in on opium sales, gold transactions, arms smuggling and other manoeuvres.*

One of the American operatives was a minor OSS officer with the unlikely name of Archimedes L.A. Patti, a major assigned to rescue Allied war prisoners. Patti did more than that. He befriended Ho Chi Minh, the wispy Vietnamese leader, who talked to him for hours, recollecting his visit to New York as a young seaman, minimizing his allegiance to Moscow and making it clear that he preferred America to the Soviet Union. Ho enlisted Patti's help in drafting his declaration of independence and sent letters of friendship through him to Washington. But Washington ignored the letters and Patti's recommendations, so that a major opportunity to cooperate with the Viet Minh and thus avoid the eventual American involvement in the Vietnam War, was lost. A chance of American recognition of Vietnam was also squandered by Prime Minister Pham Van Dong and his comrades in 1977, when US Secretary of State Cyrus Vance and President Jimmy Carter favoured such a move. However, the Vietnamese insisted, as a precondition, on some $3 billion in war reparations they said had been pledged to them by Richard Nixon, as an incentive to sign the 1973 ceasefire agreement.

Now in 1986, Vance has made a "private visit" back to Hanoi and a few mysterious Americans in Vietnam are following the luckless Patti in advocating friendship with the Vietnamese, a final end to hostilities and American recognition. While I am in Hanoi an official three-man delegation from the American Vietnam Veterans' Association is also in that city, including leader John Terzano. The association does not want its presence publicized, but is conferring with top Vietnamese officials. Its members make it clear in private conversations that they believe America should normalize relations with Vietnam and that domestic claims that the Vietnamese are still holding live MIAs is "emotional bullshit."

There is also Greg Kane, a chubby American with a boyish face, who is able, through his contacts with the Vietnamese, to bring in this first tourist group of Americans and Canadians. Kane, a left-wing radical in the sixties and seventies, was a copyboy with *Newsday*, until he was fired for trying to organize a copyboys' union. Then he led the takeover of the Statue of Liberty by the Vietnam Veterans Against the War in the early seventies and helped found the Vietnam Veterans' Association, although he served as a marine on Okinawa, not in Vietnam.

Old Asia hands learn that there is only one thing certain about the East: nothing ever is as it appears to be on the surface. And this unofficial, apparently amateur American involvement in Vietnam is mysterious.

The drive in an old, yellow Soviet-built bus from Hanoi to the main port of Haiphong is something to be experienced only once. The crumbling sixty-mile stretch of old French-built highway is North Vietnam's main road. It is a two-lane highway, but for the entire distance each side is lined with cyclists riding three abreast, young boys on water buffaloes, women bouncing along with their heavy burdens on shoulder baskets, people pulling heavy loads in carts and the occasional motorcyclist. They move one way on one side of the highway and the other way on the other side in a constant stream, so this leaves only one lane in the middle for the other constant stream of new Japanese, old Soviet and even the occasional ancient American-built trucks carrying fuel, coal, produce and people.

There are no rules of the road in North Vietnam. The trucks and the occasional bus like ours simply head straight for each other at high speeds on the single lane left available, honking their horns in a game of chicken, swerving at the very last instant to miss each other by inches and sometimes scattering the cyclists and basket-laden ladies and water buffaloes into roadside ditches. And this problem is compounded by the fact that the farmers throw thick piles of rice straw onto the centre of the highway so that the trucks will act as threshers and crushers when they run over it.

It's all so nerve-wracking it's hard to absorb the richness of the Red River Delta along the way, with women and young boys laboriously moving water from one green paddy to another in baskets or wading behind a buffalo plough. There are pretty little villages with their private plots and banana groves, and the inevitable shady "restaurant" with its single jar of cookies, a few bananas, perhaps a papaya or two, a couple of bottles of some sort of drink and cigarettes that are sold singly from the pack.

Almost every village has its own brick kiln and there are one or two red brick homes (with just a couple of small rooms each) in most of them, indicating a building boom and also backing the belief that the rush of Third World people to the urban centres has been reversed in Vietnam.

Western diplomats in Bangkok say the people are leaving the cities in droves for the villages where life is easier.

However, there seem to be no men working in these paddies or later in the quarries and coal mines on the way from Haiphong to Halong on the Gulf of Tonkin. There are some old men around in the villages, but the work is done by women and children. There are some military camps along the way and a few tanks and armoured personnel carriers behind bunkers. Presumably the young men are occupied there or are defending the border with China, not far away, where artillery attacks occur fairly frequently. Or they could be among the 150,000 Vietnamese troops fighting the Khmer Rouge in Kampuchea. Vietnam still fields the world's fourth largest army, with a strength estimated at about 1.2 million men.

All along this hazardous route, the children in the villages, the schools and paddies shout *"Lien Xo,"* which means "Russian," as we pass. More often than not they seem to shout the phrase contemptuously rather than as a greeting. They have never seen North Americans before.

But Americans seem to be distinctively preferable to the Russians. On one of the several river ferries along the way a truck hurrying to get off knocks down two tiny Vietnamese women, tangling up their shoulder baskets and scattering their loads of fruit and vegetables over the deck. Angela Giron, who is smaller even than the spread-eagled Vietnamese women, hurries to help them to their feet while I untangle the baskets and pick up the produce.

Afterwards a small boy who is with the women pats my bottom. "Okay," he says. "Americans okay."

Halong Bay, about sixty miles east of Haiphong, on the Gulf of Tonkin near the Chinese border, is one of the world's most beautiful places. The Vietnamese can take you on a boat cruise here through thousands of small, tall, jagged islands, where fishing junks sail gracefully in their hundreds. It looks like a traditional Chinese painting. But this beauty has to be earned the hard way. The hotel at Halong was an old resort for the French colonialists, and the luxurious ease of their holidays can still be imagined from the huge rooms, dining halls and balconies overlooking a white beach, with a magnificent view of the bay. Now, though, nothing works in this hotel that the Vietnamese are trying to again turn into a tourist haven. The bidet spouts a constant fountain over the floor of your bathroom. No other taps work so you have to shower with a bucket and a plastic bailer. An occasional rat runs around your room, the cockroaches are impressive and the bottled water tastes like iodine. You have to sleep under a mosquito net, but the bugs still bite. And the beach is dominated by extremely large Russian ladies in bikinis.

Apart from the natural beauty the most memorable thing about Halong Bay is a group of women coal miners, slim and tiny like most Vietnamese women, scrambling ashore from a ferry, exhausted after a day's work. It is obvious that if you scraped the black dust from their faces, they would be beautiful enough to compete with some of the West's top models. But they just sit on the dock, under their conical hats, trying to restore some strength to their frail bodies. These women earn about three hundred dong a month, worth about $1.50 on the black market. There's an overwhelming urge to walk up to one of them and give her a hundred dollars. None of us would have missed a hundred dollars much but it would, theoretically, have allowed that one, exhausted woman to take the next six years off.

Most of us have taken about five hundred dollars us in small bills into Vietnam and only managed to spend about half that amount in two weeks. That five hundred dollars has made us millionaires. In an economy that doesn't make sense, it's impossible to make valid comparisons. But, theoretically, when multipled by two hundred at the black-market rate, five hundred dollars is the equivalent of more than twenty-five years salary for a mid-level civil servant.

Bob Ringham, thirty-seven, volunteered for the US Marine Corps in 1967 because of a verbal promise on enlistment that he would become a photographer. On the last day of bootcamp he was assigned to the infantry instead and then sent to Vietnam. Now he is an award-winning photographer with the *Chicago Sun-Times* and back in Vietnam on an assignment he arranged for himself with this first group of veterans and tourists to return since the war.

As soon as I arrived in Vietnam [says Ringham] *I had orders to go up to Kaesanh. The first I saw of the country was running off the back of a C130 among mortar fire to some trenches. I was in those trenches about a week, three guys to a bunker. Then I took a helicopter up to hill 881 where my company was. I was the last guy off the helicopter and as everybody was running off they were throwing dead marines on. I stepped on the chest of a dead marine as I got off. It was a real culture shock. Nobody had taught us about that kind of death. It's not like on TV. In war people die very ugly.*

This was in January, 1968, and we didn't move off that hill for two months. We were like sitting ducks. There were fifty people in my platoon and when I got wounded on March 1 there were eight left.

Six of us were digging a new outpost when I got wounded. They dropped a mortar right into it. One fellow was killed instantly and the others were wounded above the waist. I was the only one wearing a flak jacket and I took the impact in my legs.

They couldn't get anybody in to medivac us out for two days. So we wrapped our wounds with gauze and just lay there. The shrapnel inside us was so hot when it hit us it sealed off the arteries so we didn't bleed all that much. When they tried to medivac us out after two days a sniper started firing at the guys who were carrying me on a stretcher so they dropped me and I crawled back to a bunker on my elbows. I was there for another day and then got taken to an operating theatre where they saved my legs.

When I was lying there on Hill 881, I buried a poundcake I'd been saving for my birthday and my 'C' rations, a ration card and some photographs of my parents. I always felt I had left something behind there and one reason I came back is to try to dig it up, although now I know that's impractical.

I really wanted to come back as a photographer, to see the country and photograph it because all I saw the first time was fighting and death and ugliness. And when we first arrived in Hanoi I was scared.

But now I realize how beautiful this country is and how friendly the people are. I mean they've been at war for thousands of years and we bombed the hell out of their cities and they still smile at you.

On the morning of March 8, 1965, 3,500 US marines in full battle regalia splashed ashore on the beaches of Danang, South Vietnam's second largest city, to be greeted by smiling Vietnamese girls distributing garlands of flowers and bearing a poster proclaiming: "Welcome to the Gallant Marines." If they waded ashore on these beaches today the pretty girls would still be there, but they would now be lying under colourful beach umbrellas that make the long Danang beach look a bit like an uncrowded Waikiki or Tel Aviv. It is likely they would invite the marines to the modern beach pavilion for a drink or a dance to the disco music that reverberates across the white sands.

The Marine deployment at Danang, ordered by President Lyndon Johnson in 1965, represented the first involvement of US combat troops in the Vietnam War; although it hardly rated any mention at the time, either in Congress or the American press—largely because Johnson skilfully represented it as a mere short-term expedient. It did not turn out that way. Those garlanded marines were the forerunners of nearly 200,000 US troops committed to Vietnam by the end of that year alone. That presence increased to a height of 540,000 by the end of 1968, and cost 58,000 lives and over $120 billion by the time the last American combat troops left Vietnam in 1973.

Huge airports and military bases were built in and around this central coastal city, and the American influence was felt socially here almost as strongly as in the southern capital city of Saigon. Now, twenty-one years after the marines landed only a few signs of the American military presence remain—just some Quonset huts and piles of tires and rusting metal on what were the US bases. But the social influence has lingered longer and shows in the colourful blouses of the women and in the hustle of capitalism in the well-stocked food markets. Here in Danang, and in the spiritual capital of Hue about one hundred miles away, the influence of Hanoi's socialist government obviously weakens drastically, and Vietnam starts to split into the two countries it has been for at least four decades. Most of the length of the big airstrip, where the throngs of refugees had besieged the departing planes in 1975, is closed now. It is very quiet and empty when our old Soviet jet lands and disgorges us into the terminal where AP's Peter Arnett had advised me to get out as the city collapsed and the people panicked.

Though the streets of the city are bustling, they seem to me to be strangely uncrowded. I ask at the Oriental Hotel, a fairly modern structure in the Soviet style, for directions to the Grande Hotel where we few remaining correspondents had spent that last nervous night before the Communists came—but nobody has heard of it. So I walk the quiet and empty docks until I find a big, old gray building. The doors the owner had locked as I left years ago are open and the building seems to be a combination of market place at ground level and living quarters for scores of families above. I ask several people at the doorway, in English and French, whether this had been the Grande Hotel and they shrug their shoulders. They've never heard, they say, of any Grande Hotel or of the woman who used to own it.

Tim Manigan, a public affairs aide to the governor of Rhode Island, was one of the 200,000 US combat troops who followed the small group of marines into Vietnam in 1967. Now, nineteen years later, he sits on the beach at Danang, the deep scars of an ugly wound showing in his side, and he talks about the war:

I was drafted into the army in 1967 and I was doing reconnaisance with the Twenty-fifth Infantry Division during the Tet Offensive in March, 1968 [Manigan says]. *I was working with an infantry division known as the Wolf-hounds around the village of Hoc Mon about half way between Cuchi and Saigon.*

On March 14, we started moving onto the treeline on the outskirts of the village. We didn't know it but we'd stumbled on a very large unit of Viet Cong.

Hoc Mon turned out to be a training site and the unit there had a lot to do with the Tet invasion of Saigon and they were slowly moving northwest to try to go back to Cambodia. We thought this village was relatively secure. It wasn't, though. We stumbled across a tremendous amount of resistance. There was a lot of rocket fire and our tanks were being hit. We were unable to penetrate very far into the treeline and there was a heavy exchange of fire all day long. There were a lot killed and wounded.

So about 4 p.m. they asked me to do a recon around the other side of the village. We moved around the other side in an armoured personnel carrier, just the driver and me, and we were able to advance maybe 150 yards into the treeline. But three members of the Wolfhounds had got there before us and into an area where there was an old French cemetery. This cemetery was surrounded by a wall about a foot and a half high and they were pinned down there by some heavy machine-gun fire. So I got up on top of the APC and I said to the driver, "Why don't we go over there and pick up those three guys?"

The lieutenant in my unit told me on the radio not to go. We were under a lot of rocket fire and were losing tanks and APCs. Finally I switched the radio off and just out of conscience I felt I couldn't go without those three guys. I had a 50-calibre machine-gun up there and I fired a three-hundred-round ammunition belt to lay down some ground cover and we picked them up. But as soon as the

fifty-cal belt ran out a Viet Cong up to my left in the shrub-
bery let go with an entire clip of ammunition from an AK
47 rifle. One or two bullets—they never knew—passed
through the left side of my body and out my back. I
lowered myself down the main hatch of the personnel car-
rier. I was bleeding.

They got me to Japan where I had four operations in
four months. Then I had more operations when I got back
to the States.

I was happy to be home, of course, but it didn't take
me long to realize that when I had been away in Vietnam
there had been a great attitude shift.

Americans had supported the war when I went. But
when I came back you couldn't find anybody who did.
They all said they were always against it. It's not that peo-
ple hated me for being there. It was more that they were
embarrassed. When I'd go to a party a hush would fall
over the room. People didn't dislike me. They just disliked
talking about the war.

I was twenty-one when I came home. It was very diffi-
cult for me.

And we were all stereotyped. People remembered
seeing on the news that vets were drug addicts or they
were fragging each other and I felt real bad because I was
there with the best young men that America could send,
who performed admirably and did a good job. The war
was not lost by the American troops in Vietnam. It was lost
back home.

I'm back here now because I had to come back. Viet-
nam changed my life. It made me a better person. Every
day I live now is a plus and I try to do something special
every day. I made an investment of myself in Vietnam and
coming back is a bit like coming back to the old neigh-
bourhood where you were raised. I grew up here in Viet-

nam. So I had to come back and take just one last look at it and maybe put it to rest.

There is no violence in Vietnam now. The countryside is as peaceful as a pale watercolour. You have to travel a long way to see even the remnants of past violence, like the occasional rusting tank in a field, or you have to go to Hanoi where there is a war museum with parts of American B-52s and captured tanks and guns on display along with pictures of downed American pilots. If there was agent orange around it is, of course, not obvious. If the forests were hit by napalm they have grown again.

The citadel at Hue, where the marines fought so desperately in 1967 is intact and preserved, and is still one of the world's most beautiful structures. It is not just one forbidding-looking fortress as it appears to be in pictures, but a whole succession of guilded buildings that hide one behind the other, and are more beautiful and mysterious than the Forbidden City in Beijing. Young men are playing an apparently important soccer match in the field in front of the citadel while we are there, while Big John, the ex-marine who fought at the citadel, sits alone in our battered Russian tour bus with tears rolling down his cheeks.

The country was violent when I was here the last time in 1975. The Vietnamese were killing themselves at a rate of about ten thousand a month. But now war is confined to the occasional artillery attacks across the border with China, and we haven't seen that. The only sign of violence I have seen is a grandma flailing a young boy with a buffalo whip on a village road outside Hue. She has slashed the howling kid nine times when I turn away. The way she is hitting him he must have done something terrible. Otherwise, wherever we go the Vietnamese countryside is, to me and the American vets, almost awesomely peaceful.

Saigon's main street used to be Rue Catinat. Then it became Tu Do Street which means "freedom." Now it's Dong Knoi Street, which means "uprising." But it could be the main street of the world. The French brought some culture and civility to this fairly narrow, tree-lined artery that stretches for not much more than a mile through the centre of hot, sprawling Ho Chi Minh City. The Americans provided a big dose of money, brashness and sin to Tu Do in the 1960s. Then when Saigon fell in 1975, the Communist North Vietnamese added strict ideology and discipline. So the street most people still call Tu Do in the downtown area of Ho Chi Minh City—still officially called Saigon, just as Manhattan is part of New York City—is a street with a little bit of everything. It even has some class, with its fine old opera house and magnificent Catholic cathedral. Now European, American and Asian cultures compete uncomfortably on this symbolic street, along with capitalism and communism. Capitalism is winning.

Ten years after the war, in 1985, two out of three of the street's stores were closed, grilles pulled shut and windows boarded over when their owners fled to France or the United States in the months before the city fell. Now, in 1986, two out of three of the stores are open, although the goods they offer, mostly jewellry and laquerware, can't compete with the variety of electronic and other imported goods in the black market a few blocks away. On this colourful main street now, as ever, commerce and chicanery mix with beggars and thieves, who can cut the strap of a camera bag or lift a watch as professionally as anywhere in the world. Catholic nuns and Buddhist monks mingle with Communist cadres, money changers, "cowboys" in jeans and American T-shirts and an occasional pretty girl in a traditional *ao dai.*

The Honda motorcycles that screamed in their constant hundreds along Tu Do when the Americans were here are mostly gone now. The working girls who plied their trade so aggressively in clubs, on corners and at places like the rooftop bar of the Miramar Hotel have done their time in the Communist re-education camps, learning basket weaving or something socially useful. The daughters of some are said to be active these days, but they're not obvious.

The noisy Hondas have been replaced by bicycles and three-wheeled cyclos. There are no taxis on Tu Do, or anywhere in the city, and even the few remaining motorized cyclos are used only for cargoes of rice sacks, coal or dead pigs—except, amazingly on Sunday nights. Then, in a weird time warp, scores of Hondas, using preciously saved black-market gas, suddenly appear with good-looking young women on the pillions. They roar down Tu Do and up adjacent Nguyen Hue Street, around and around this circuit in a sort of ceremonial reminder of the way things once were. The display draws so many thousands of envious couples on bicycles to the sidewalks and roadsides that police have to constantly plough through them in trucks to clear a way for the motorcyclists.

The old 1950s Chevs and Plymouths that used to carry correspondents to the "bang bangs" are parked in a row on Nguyen Hue Street, all painted and gussied up and used, we are told, only for weddings now. I searched among them for my old driver and friend Hughie, whose amazing instinct for survival used to make him dive into ditches minutes before incoming shells even started to whistle in the sky. But the drivers were all younger than Hughie would have been now. They'd never heard of him.

The last time I had walked down Tu Do Street on that April day in 1975, after the big barrage hit the airport and the city rumbled, the street was eerily empty except for me and the flower-girl who said "bye bye." Now, as an alleged tourist, I walk back up Tu Do on the route I took so many times to the Reuter news agency's office. Mostly it is like walking with ghosts.

The "Bank of India" is still open, despite time and communism. It is a little variety store, called the Majestic Store, next to the Majestic Hotel, where two Indian brothers changed money at decent black-market rates for correspondents and others for years. Now only the younger brother is there, welcoming someone he vaguely recognizes. "My brother became very rich and went to Australia," he says. "But me and my wife remain. You want to change money?—two hundred [dong] to the dollar." The cashier's wicket at the back of the store where the money is changed is still in full view of anyone who enters the place. A picture of Indian Prime Minister Rajiv Gandhi has been hung next to one of his late mother, Indira. And, of course, there is also a picture of Ho Chi Minh for good measure. The official exchange rate is fifteen dong to the dollar so the two hundred rate is, as usual, fair enough. But how the Bank of India has managed to survive the changing ideologies is one of Saigon's many mysteries.

There are a couple of young women in tight jeans in the bar next door to the Bank of India, but they are not rattling on the windows as they used to after the Americans left. And there are persistent beggars on the street, mostly youngsters, a few of them black with fair hair. At the Miramar Hotel, the woman at the reception desk says the rooftop bar is closed now and the hotel is full of Soviets.

"Russians number ten," she says, pointing both thumbs downwards. "Most of the other rooftop girls have gone to the States," she explains, indicating that she was one of them, "but I couldn't go because I had to look after my parents." She wants to chat longer. It's obvious she misses the old days.

The shop of Minh the tailor, where Neil Davis bought the last of the bush jackets, is just as he described it, still shuttered, with the grilles drawn. In fact, there are no tailor shops for men on Tu Do now, where once there were at least ten. Now there are just a few shops with rolls of colourful material in the windows for making *ao dais*. The maitre d' at the rooftop restaurant of the Caravelle, where I always stayed, is still there. But he's not anxious to talk about the days before the Communists came. "Some other correspondents came back last year," he volunteers quietly. "But it's not the same here now as it used to be." He sees people watching us talk and walks away.

On the terrace of the Continental Palace Hotel I sit at a table I think is the one where Graham Greene wrote most of *The Quiet American*. The place is partly boarded up now, but you can still buy a cold, good Saigon beer. I was the only one there. No girls now. No crowds and chatter. Ti Ti, the tiny, raggedy jasmine girl is, of course, not there any more and Con Cua ("The Crab") has gone from the pavement. But their places have been taken by a new generation of less colourful beggars on the street outside the terrace, and there are skinny men already preparing on this early evening to sleep on the pavement.

Tu Do is quiet. The real action now is in the few narrow, crowded, nearby streets of the black market. Here small stores and street stalls are packed with almost every electronic appliance imaginable and with imported toiletries that range from toothpaste to expensive perfumes. Pri-

224

ces are marked, so there is no haggling. A small Sony ghetto blaster costs 45,000 dong ($3,000 at the official exchange rate) and a 25-inch Hitachi colour TV is marked at 390,000 dong ($26,000). Even at the current black-market rate of two hundred to the dollar the set is expensive, the equivalent of $1,950. And a block off Tu Do—beyond where the big statue of the Vietnamese marine once stood and where the Buddhist monks used to set themselves on fire—the top floor of the Rex Hotel jumps and jives a few nights a week. It used to be the US Officers' Club. Now it's a dance hall, with loud music that ranges from Doris Day songs to hard rock, with some Irish and Soviet melodies thrown in. Its dance floor is packed with women in tight western dress who look as if they failed the Communist re-education course for street girls, but also with demure-looking young ladies in *ao dai*, dancing mostly with Soviet men. It costs the equivalent of twenty-five cents for admission, fifty cents for a beer, and fifty-five cents for a dance. The girls suddenly disappear, like a bunch of Cinderellas, exactly at the stroke of midnight but it is said that in some instances "arrangements can be made."

When I left Vietnam as Saigon fell at the end of the war, I wrote that "Saigon had seduced the French and led the Americans astray. It is a whore of a city that will one day even corrupt the Communists." I was right about that, but not quite yet.

Tu Do Street is not Vietnam [says Chuck Porzelt, who used to skipper a patrol boat on the Mekong River]. *The real Vietnam is out there in the villages where all the people really want is a patch of land and some peace to cultivate it.*

*I got close to the people when I was on the Mekong
and I came to love and respect them. We pulled in to a lot
of villages and hamlets and the people were friendly, nice.
I mean, it's a totally different world out there to what you
deal with in the cities.*

*It was rough in the river patrol boats, but it was not
like it was in the film* Apocalypse Now. *That was unreal.
We were never really sure where we were operating and
we were under fire a lot in our 25-foot launches from
armed sampans and land ambushes. I killed some Viet
Cong and this was close-up killing. You could see who you
were shooting. But at the time I didn't really stop to think
about it.*

*I think I came back for different reasons to the others
on this trip. I always knew I wanted to come back one day
because of the people and the beautiful countryside. I had
to see what it was like now.*

*I felt very strange when we first landed in Hanoi. But
I didn't sense any animosity. There seemed to be no hard
feelings on the part of the people at all. Now America
should also realize that the war is over and recognize Vietnam. I suppose everything we do in America is done because it is of benefit to us. But we can help these people at
the same time as we help ourselves. If we helped them economically it would help stabilize this whole Southeast
Asian area.*

*A lot of American servicemen thought Tu Do Street
was Vietnam. But it's not, you know. Vietnam is out there
in the hamlets and villages.*

In my years of covering Asia I always avoided, as much as
possible, the use of the rickshaw or the cyclo because there

seems to be a lack of human dignity in having one ill-fed man exerting himself in the heat on behalf of a well-fed one. And now in Ho Chi Minh City, where you either use cyclos or walk, this uncomfortable feeling increases because some of the hundreds of cyclos who circle the streets and clog the corners in search of fares that amount to the equivalent of a few cents for a long journey, are intellectuals who were on the wrong side of the war.

One evening Angela Giron, the tiny actress and aspiring novelist from our group, hails a cyclo outside the Majestic Hotel to take her to a tailor shop where she had ordered an *ao dai*. The cyclo speaks perfect French, as Angela does because she lives in Montreal, and as he certainly should because he taught the language at Saigon University before the Communists came. He tells Angie she is the first Western woman he's ever pedalled and the first ever to converse with him in French, and he invites her to have a cup of coffee with him. She is concerned for her safety, of course, but she judges that the cyclo is trying to regain some of the dignity he had lost long ago, and decides to go with him.

The cyclo takes her to a little restaurant that is heavily grilled so they won't be noticed from the street, and he treats her with old-world gallantry. He insists on paying for the coffees. At one stage, as they chat in French, a pathetically-skinny drug addict, his arm pockmarked by needles, crawls miserably on his stomach across the floor of the little restaurant with his hand outstretched to the cyclo. The cyclo gives him ten dong, the equivalent of a few cents. The North American woman cannot get over the fact that the poor cyclo would help someone even worse off than himself. When she comes back to the big, comfortable, canopied seats in the bar of the Majestic and tells us the story, she begins to sob uncontrollably.

I am taking a cyclo this morning because I've had a few shivers and think I might have malaria and need to go to a hospital. He takes me to a pediatric research centre, but that is OK. There is a doctor there who speaks good English and perfect French. While we are waiting for the results of a blood test (which is negative) the doctor sits beside me on a balcony and talks quietly. He says he had been educated in France, received his medical degree there thirty years ago, and had been a major in the South Vietnamese army when Saigon fell. Then he spent three years in re-education camp outside Dalat doing hard and menial labour.

"After that I tried to escape in a boat once but didn't make it," he says. "But I'm not too badly off. A lot of my colleagues are still in re-education." He said he is being paid 250 dong a month, which is the equivalent of about $1.55, for his work at the pediatric research centre. He expresses considerable professional satisfaction in his job because there is much malnutrition in the country and some starvation. He says the malnutrition is drastically weakening the resistance of many children against other serious afflictions like malaria and the plague.

I tell him many doctors in North America are earning well over $100,000 a year and complaining that it is not enough. I offer to give him a few dollars to help him along, but he refuses, looking about him as if the balcony posts have ears. He has to charge me forty dong (a few cents) for the pills he gives me and, as I pay that in his office I slip a ten dollar bill under a notepad on his desk. I hope he finds it. On the black market it is worth eight month's salary for a skilled and highly civilized doctor in Saigon.

At Tan Son Nhut airport on the way home I am supposed to be thinking, for the sake of the series of stories I am writing for *The Star*, about the last time I left Saigon. I remember how we reached the airport in the crowded, gray bus and the panicky people pounding on its doors when we stopped. I recall the plane crash in Cholon just as we reached the airport and the shell hitting the tarmac as we pulled in to the Pentagon East, while Peter Collins, the cbs correspondent, shouted "Oh, my God, not here, not now." I remember the red flare that stopped my heart as the big chopper zig-zagged to gain height because I thought it was a heat-seeking missile. I also think of the captain of the *Denver* who kicked me off his ship because I wasn't American, and the six days on that crowded, thirsty freighter on the South China Sea.

But that was then and this is now. Now, as we walk onto the tarmac at Tan Son Nhut to take a bus to a gleaming white Air France 747, a huge crowd packing the terminal's balconies begins wailing as if the end of the world was upon them. I climb onto one bus with three of the American veterans of our group and find it full of teenagers, mostly girls, wailing in the same way. Their tears are splashing onto the leather seats of the bus, creating pools, and some of the youngsters are flailing their arms and tugging their hair in emotional agony.

I ask a man at the front of the bus what is going on. "These are Amerasian children." he says. "This is part of the American Orderly Departure Program. They'll be going to the States in a little while."

"Well," I say stating the very obvious, "they don't seem to want to go."

The wailing of the Vietnamese mothers and grandparents on the airport balconies and the tears of the youngsters are contagious. "This is sad," says Big John Raths, the ex-marine. "I mean we're talking really sad here. I've never seen anything so sad." And he takes off his glasses and wipes them, as tears start streaming down his rugged face. Chuck Porzelt, who skippered the patrol boat on the Mekong, and Tim Manigan, who was so badly wounded near Saigon, begin to cry.

And even this old correspondent weeps a little, not just for the kids but for a beautiful country that is sad all over.

XIV

The End of a Legend

AFTER NEIL DAVIS, the baby-faced, Tasmanian television cameraman and correspondent, took the pictures of the Communist tanks crashing through the palace gates in Saigon in 1975, he remained in the conquered city for about six months then went about his business of covering wars everywhere. From his base in Bangkok he went to the Sudan, Lebanon, the Philippines, Zaire, Angola, Uganda, Zimbabwe, the Yemens, Iran and Iraq, where he was imprisoned for a week as a suspected spy. In many of the campaigns he wore the cream-coloured bush jacket from Mr. Minh's in Saigon.

Before the fall of Saigon, Davis was already the correspondent the other correspondents respected and admired most. While more than eighty fellow newsmen had died in Indochina, he had defied the odds almost daily since he first arrived in Vietnam in 1964, a year before the US Marines landed in Danang. He worked then for Visnews,

231

the London-based TV news agency, as a cameraman-corre-
spondent and he chose to concentrate on South Vietnamese troops in action, rather than the Americans because, as he put it, "It was their war. It meant a great deal
to them."

He was a front-line man. While some of us with much
less experience covered the wars some of the time from
the rooftops of hotels or even sometimes by employing
courageous "natives" for a few dollars to report back to us
from the front, Davis was always in the thick of it himself.
But he approved of the careful correspondent. "You're nuts
if you go out there, mate," he told me once in Cambodia.
"You can get your story just as easily here in the hotel and
on the streets. There's no sense in risking both our necks
and I'll tell you what's going on when I get back. I'm stuck
with this bloody camera so I've got to go anyway. Have you
got a cigarette, mate?"

Another time he said: "I always try to go to the extreme front line. You can't get the spontaneity of action if
you are not there. You can't get it if you're a hundred
metres behind the soldiers trying to get it with a telephoto
lens. You don't see the faces, the expressions. You don't
feel the compassion that they may show for their wounded
comrades, or for their enemy for that matter." And when
asked once why he did what he did, he replied: "It's exciting, that's obvious, mate, and it gets a bit boring to be anywhere else. But nobody likes to be shot at."

He had no death wish. In fact, he was probably the
most careful of all of the correspondents, constantly weigh-
ing the value of the story against the risks required to get
it. "Not down here, mate, not today," he frequently told
companions. "I don't like the look of this." When he went
into the bush in Cambodia or Vietnam he always went first
with the veterans. "When you are green never go alone,"

he advised the less experienced correspondents who tried to emulate him. "Learn from the old pros. It may save your life. If you hear a crack, hit the ground. When you see vegetation freshly cut, suspect an ambush, suspect minefields. Don't think, act. You've got to perfect your ability to hit the ground."

Still, despite his professional carefulness, the wars left fifteen scars on his body. There were metal fragments imbedded permanently in his index finger, in his right shin bone and in his back. His closest shave occurred in 1974 outside Phnom Penh, when a chunk of shrapnel came close to tearing through his guts but was partially blocked by a tape recorder strapped to his waist. His greatest fear was of a massive wound that would leave him both alive and crippled.

Davis took many memorable pictures, some of which changed the course of wars. He took the shot of Saigon Police General Loan executing a young Viet Cong, the pistol to his head, on Tryang Hung Dao Avenue in Saigon during the 1968 Tet Offensive. After the world uproar the picture caused he met Loan again in Hue. Loan pointed a machine pistol at Davis and said, "Davis, someday I'll shoot you." "Of course," Davis said, "he was joking."

Before the My Lai massacre he took dramatic shots of Americans mowing down a Viet Cong under a flag of truce, a sequence that was featured in a film about Davis called *Frontline*, which placed second in the documentary section of the 1981 Academy Awards. "His intention was clear," Davis said of the Viet Cong with the white flag, "but a GI commanded, 'Bullshit! Cut him down! Cut him down!'" A burst of gunfire ended the dramatic film sequence.

Davis was there when the rocket attack hit outside the Monorom Hotel in Phnom Penh, just before the city's fall, killing eight or ten pedicab drivers. He can be seen in black-and-white pictures I took from the opposite side of the scene, camera on shoulder, calmly doing his job. His colour film of that ugly desolation provided the real life and shocking beginning of the film, *The Killing Fields*.

Yet fame eluded him. He didn't want it anyway. He didn't like the "glory boys" who rushed out from the US or other countries with little knowledge of, or feel for, the East or experience of war, in order to make a quick name for themselves. They were dangerous, he believed, to themselves and others. "If you must do it, do it not because you want to be famous," he advised at least one greenhorn. "That's the way most journalists die, when they go for a big kill with a show of excessive bravado." And he was quietly and philosophically peeved after NBC sent him back into Vietnam for two months in 1985 for a major story in connection with the tenth anniversary of the fall of Saigon. He wrote and filmed the story and it was his expertise, compassion and understanding that made it successful. But, typically, NBC sent some of what Davis used to call the "pretty boys" from New York to do the on-camera work and gain all the glory.

Kevin Hamilton, managing editor of Visnews Ltd., the television agency Davis first worked for in Indochina, said of him:

There is a great rivalry amongst journalists, and Neil Davis was as competitive as any of us. But there is also, within the news community, a bond that transcends competition, born perhaps out of shared experience, some of it dangerous, some of it not. Neil Davis, in his years in Asia, first with Visnews and then with NBC, was a shining example of what that bond is all about. Were he in show business, he would inevitably have been described by the cliché writers as a legend in his own lifetime. But I doubt if that's the way Neil saw himself. He loved Asia and its people and he loved showing them to the world, warts and all, in the way he knew best. He quickly came to the understanding that the way to cover wars and violence for television was to be up front, where the wars and violence are evident. No soft aftermath pics for Davis; that wasn't his way. But whatever the legendmakers might say, Neil was neither rash nor foolhardy, nor did he have anything resembling a death wish. He was totally professional under fire, always calculating the odds, always using that sixth sense that comes with experience. When amateurs and newcomers to war latched themselves onto him, as they often did, he would invariably back off to protect them from themselves. He wanted the story, yes, but not at the expense of life—his own included.

In more recent times, as he covered the wars from Africa to Iran and Iraq, Davis was to some extent illogically driven by a sense of shame for having abandoned his beloved Cambodia in the American helicopter evacuation of Phnom Penh—"Operation Eagle Pull"—shortly before the city fell, while others like Jon Swain, Sydney Schanberg and Al Rockoff had remained. "Bloody humiliating, mate," he used to say when he referred to this escape. And he vowed never to run away from a story again. Mostly, though, he was driven by professionalism. Wars were his business and he was a front-line man. But he was more than a craftsman with a camera. Over the years he acquired knowledge that made him an authority on armies, military hardware and battle tactics. He had a deep understanding of the history, geography and culture of Indochina, especially Cambodia. Not only journalists, but generals frequently sought his advice and ambassadors begged for his guidance.

Davis continued to watch as the Cambodian war continued and was forgotten in the United States and
elsewhere, and as Prince Sihanouk and an old Cambodian
nationalist and former prime minister named Son Sann
formed an unholy alliance with the despicable Pol Pot.
They fought guerrilla battles against the Vietnamese who in
1978 had occupied Cambodia, now Kampuchea, and forci-
bly, most thought mercifully, deposed Pol Pot and the Organization on High. Davis sometimes sneaked back over
the border to advise Son Sann on military tactics and politics because he thought the old man might be the saviour
of his beloved, adopted land. There were times, some who
went with him said, when malaria hit him on the difficult
way and he had to be helped through the jungle to sit at
the camp tables of the Son Sann guerrillas to dispense his
advice. And there were colleagues who, rightly, repri-
manded him for this obvious loss of journalistic objectivity.
But they forgave him because he was Davis, whom they
nicknamed "The Fox," and he brought them back knowledge and information.

They knew that as a correspondent and cameraman he
was, in fact, two men and sometimes he was three, because
in dangerous situations he often dispensed with a soundman and did that job as well. He was the ultimate commu-
nicator at the start of the new information era. His pre-
decessors in Victorian times, the Irishman William Howard
Russell, the first and greatest of the war correspondents,
and the American Henry Morton Stanley and their colleagues, who covered fewer wars at a more leisurely pace,
would have been both proud of his efforts and envious of
his heavy, modern technological equipment that allowed
him to tell the story so much better and quicker than they
could. They might also have wondered why this quiet-spo-
ken, slightly-built and frequently malaria-stricken successor

236

of theirs did not have porters to carry his heavy gear or at least a mule or two for his whisky and personal effects.

But Davis was one of them. He drank his share and although he was supposed to have stopped smoking it was a constant joke that he had only stopped smoking his own. Women loved him and he loved them back in large numbers. His Buddhist instincts, a legacy of his long time in Cambodia, caused him often to proclaim that death was a lady who greets you softly. "If she's a lady," his irreverent Australian colleagues would reply, "then you've probably met her already and screwed her." He'd been a professional Australian Rules football player in his youth and despite the bouts with malaria, he kept himself fit at fifty-one years of age for his dangerous jobs in the wars, and his amourous liaisons at home, by running miles around the Bangkok parks and playing tennis matches on which he bet considerable amounts. He'd bet on anything but especially cricket test matches, which he loved, and boxing, on which he was an expert.

He was also the patriarch of a group of wandering correspondents based in Bangkok that came to be called the Australian Mafia, although its ranks included New Zealanders, Britons and Americans. They were a wild bunch when at home, likely to be found as often chatting around the small bar beneath the stageful of dancing girls at the American-owned Grand Prix nightclub on notorious Patpong Road, as in the plush Foreign Correspondents' Club on the top floor of the Dusit Thani Hotel. Despite this, however, Davis was elected president of the Foreign Correspondents' Club in 1982. It was an interesting administrative period described by more sombre club members as "The Year of Living Dangerously."

In the early morning hours of Monday, September 9, 1985, Davis was tipped by some of his many contacts that

an attempted coup by former Supreme Military Commander General Serm na Nakhon and a few followers was
under way in Bangkok. It was not much of an attempted
coup in a city that saw many of them and unless it was successful, which was unlikely, it would make only a few seconds of air time in the United States, if it made any time at
all. It was just another crappy little coup in Thailand.

Davis called his soundman, Bill Latch, an American,
and they grabbed their equipment and made their way to
the First Army Division headquarters on Rajdamnern Avenue where a small group of rebels had briefly taken over
the radio station, General Serm had announced the dissolu-
tion of parliament and the government and renounced the
constitution.

The rebels inside the radio station were soon over-
powered by loyal troops under Deputy Army Commander-
in-Chief General Thienchai Sirisamphan who issued a
counter-coup announcement shortly after 9 a.m., stating
that government troops had the situation in hand and that
General Serm had contacted the government side asking to
surrender. But by then three rebel-held M-41 tanks had
lined up on nearby Phitsanuloke Road, their guns trained at
the radio station, a nest of machine guns behind them.

Davis and Latch were standing in front of two telephone booths immediately to the right of the radio station
gates when the tank machine gunners opened fire without
warning from the other side of the street. They hit the
ground and were forced to stay there for about a minute
until there was a lull in the shooting. Then, crouching low,
they ran along the footpath to join Australian Visnews cameraman Gary Burns and his Thai soundman Daeng Kariah
who had taken cover behind a post-office box and a roadside tree.

Burns was a protégé of Davis and one of his closest

friends. They had met in London in 1973 when Davis was on leave from Cambodia. Davis had taken him to dinner. "That long, boozy dinner was to alter the course of my life," Burns used to say. "It was the night that led me to making the decision to follow in Neil's footsteps and seek a correspondent/cameraman's posting with Visnews. That decision led to twelve years of Neil's friendship and guidance, and salad days in Africa and Asia when life was so sweet we just knew we would all live forever. Neil was what I wanted to be when I grew up."

The lull in the shooting did not last long. The tanks started to fire their main 76-millimetre cannon in addition to their turret-mounted .50 calibre machine guns. The fire was almost continuous, but the newsmen were professionally sheltered in the cover of the post-office box and tree, still rolling film. Then two shells exploded against a wall behind the two television crews. Davis was nearest the point of impact and shrapnel tore into his side causing massive wounds. Shrapnel also shattered Latch's ankle and splattered his back. The head of a machine gun bullet ricocheted off the concrete, entered his rib cage, bisected his liver and left Latch mortally wounded.

Davis dived on top of Burns to protect him and twice Burns asked him, "Are you hit, are you hit?" And twice Davis replied, "I'm all right, mate." Then he said, "Oh, shit!" and he died.

In the tradition of the combat cameraman he kept his camera rolling to record his own death.

Index

Index

United Press International (UPI), 23, 121, 123, 147

Vance, Cyrus, 209
Van Zyl, Mike, 168, 169, 178, 180
Viet Cong, 18, 19, 25, 26, 35, 36, 46, 131, 137, 143, 150-152, 218, 219, 226, 233
Viznews, 125, 231, 234, 238, 239
Vogle, Paul, 111, 121
Voice of America, 207

Walker, John, 23, 26

Wallace, Edgar, xxii
Warner, Denis, 53
Washington Post, 157, 159
Westminster Gazette, xvi
Wilkinson-Latham, Robert, xiv, xx
Wilson, Bruce, 114, 121
Wilson, Ian, 128, 137
World Airways, 115, 119-122
World War I, xiv, xxii, xxiii
World War II, xiv, xxii, xxiii, 8, 15, 74, 82, 157, 167, 199